handball-uebungen.de
Trainingseinheiten und Übungen für Ihr Training!

I0220734

Table of contents:

Introduction

Publishing Information
1st English edition released on 14 Nov 2018
German original edition released on 23 Aug 2016

Published by DV Concept
Editors, design, and layout: Jörg Madinger, Elke Lackner
Proofreading and English translation: Nina-Maria Nahlenz

ISBN: 978-3-95641-235-6

This publication is listed in the catalogue of the **German National Library**. Please refer to http://dnb.de for bibliographic data.

Introduction

Dear reader

Thank you for choosing a book of the handball-uebungen.de training guide series.

Fast breaks are an important factor for successful handball game outcomes in modern handball. Further positive aspects include motivation of the team through quick goals in connection with demoralization of the opposing team as well as improvement of the attractiveness of the handball game itself. Quick adjustment from defense to offense play after winning the ball (or after a fast throw-off following a goal) in order to take advantage of the off-guard situation and score a goal through increased speed of play is the central objective of speed play with fast breaks.

From winning the ball and
- quickly adjusting from defense to offense play
- to initiating the first or subsequent second wave
- and a well-structured action following the second wave
- or the fast throw-off
all these fast break elements are dealt with during the following five training units.

The first two units focus on fast break initiation and the improvement of passing precision and passing decisions for a first wave as well as carrying the ball forward after gaining ball possession. The third unit focuses on the decision-making process in outnumbered situations that may be created during the first or second wave, whereas the last two units practice well-structured playing against an off-guard and passively acting defense formation.

With these five training units, the collection offers ideas and incentives for practicing the individual fast break phases and provides the opportunity to implement a comprehensive concept that involves both the first and second wave and the fast throw-off.

This book contains the following training units:

TU 1 – Improving passing precision when initiating the first wave (★★)

The objective of this training unit is to improve running paths, passing and the decision-making process during the first wave. After a warm-up running exercise, the subsequent short game already includes quick adjustment exercises and long passes. During the ball familiarization phase and the goalkeeper warm-up shooting, the players practice playing long passes before they combine several actions with first wave initiation in a series of shots. The closing small group exercises finally focus on making passing decisions.

TU 2 – Quick adjustment to a fast break after a defense action (★★★)

The objective of this training unit is to practice the quick adjustment from defense play to fast break initiation. Following the warm-up phase with a coordination run exercise and the ball familiarization phase, the goalkeeper warm-up shooting combines a preparatory defense exercise and a series of shots for the goalkeeper. During the two subsequent defense exercises, the players practice quick adjustment from defense work to fast break countermovement. A 4-on-4 game and a sprint contest complete this training unit.

TU 3 – Improving speed play for fast break situations (★★★)

The objective of this training unit is to improve free play in fast break situations. Following warm-up and a short game, the players play long passes during the ball familiarization phase which will be further developed in the goalkeeper warm-up shooting exercise. This is followed by a series of shots requiring precise passes. Afterwards, the players practice free play in outnumbered, open situations during fast breaks. A closing game with gradually increasing complexity completes this training unit.

TU 4 – Developing a well-structured second wave by implementing long crossing moves and options for further playing (★★★)

The objective of this training unit is to develop a long crossing during the second wave. Following a warm-up running exercise, a short game, and a ball familiarization exercise, the players initially develop the long crossing during the goalkeeper warm-up shooting phase. In the subsequent series of shots which will be combined with a 1-on-0 fast break, the players practice the long crossing with compensation of the center back player. Defense players and the pivot are added for the two subsequent small group exercises, before the players implement the course 4-on-4 during the closing part of the training unit.

TU 5 – Step-by-step development of initial actions after a fast throw-off (★★★)

The objective of this training unit is to develop a simple initial action after a fast throw-off. Following warm-up and a coordination run exercise, the players practice the basics during the ball familiarization phase and the goalkeeper warm-up shooting. During the three subsequent exercises, the players further develop the running and passing paths and eventually combine them in order to create an initial action. In the closing game, the players implement what they practiced before.

Training unit requirements:

★   Simple requirement (all youth and adult teams)

★ ★   Intermediate requirement (youth teams under 15 years of age and adult teams)

★ ★ ★   Higher requirement (youth teams under 17 years of age and adult teams)

★ ★ ★ ★   Highest requirements (competitive area)

1. Insight into the annual schedule

Training objectives
In the training of **adult teams**, a coach usually will be measured based on his or her success (league position). Hence, the individual training units are strongly focused on the respective opposing team (aim of season). Winning games and making efficient use of the team's potential are paramount.

In the training of **youth teams**, however, the **individual development** is the most important objective which has priority over success. The players should also be trained on a general basis, i.e. on each position (no positional specialization, no offense/defense specialization).

Fast breaks play an important role in both areas. Especially for youth teams with their offensively acting defense formations, playing the first wave, carrying the ball forward quickly, and adjusting to outnumbered situations during the fast break play a crucial role.
With increasing age, comprehensive fast break concepts with a well-structured second wave become more and more important.

Annual schedule
The following points should be taken into consideration when creating your annual schedule:
- How many training units do I have (do not forget vacations, holidays, and the season schedule)?
- What do I want to achieve/improve this season?
- What goals should be achieved within a given concept (of the club, the association, i.e. the German Handball Association [DHB], for example)? You can refer to the publications of the DHB for information about defense systems, individual offense/defense skills, and the expected performance of a certain age group.
- What skills does my team have (do the individual players have)? You should continuously analyze and document the skills of your team so that you can make a target-performance comparison at a regular basis.

Annual schedule

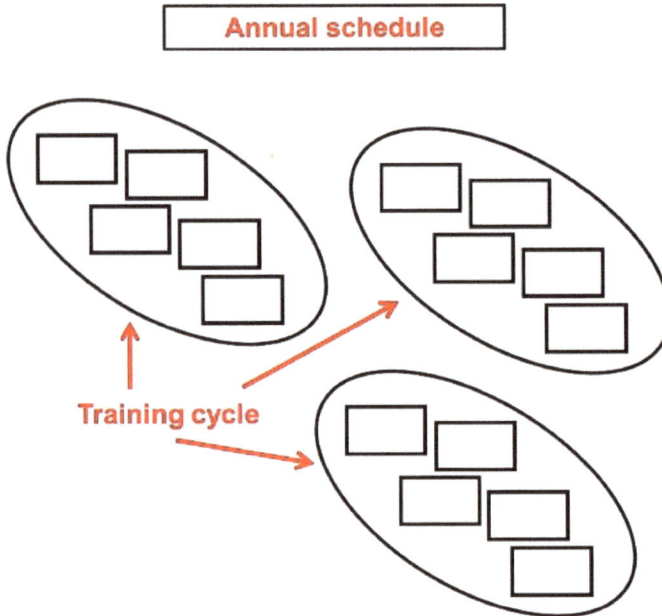

Training cycle

Individual steps of the annual schedule

A handball season can be divided into the following training phases:

- Preparatory phase until the first game: This phase is suitable for improving physical fitness skills such as endurance.
- 1st part of the season until the Christmas holidays: The Christmas break should be kept in mind here.
- 2nd part of the season until the end of season.

You should then refine and elaborate these training phases step by step.

- Division of training phases into sections with part-specific objectives (monthly schedule, e.g.).
- Division into weekly schedules.
- Planning of individual training units.

Training cycle

Training unit:
→ Warm-up
→ Basic exercise
→ Basic play
→ Target play

Training unit:
→ Warm-up
→ Basic exercise
→ Basic play
→ Target play

Training unit:
→ Warm-up
→ Basic exercise
→ Basic play
→ Target play

Training unit:
→ Warm-up
→ Basic exercise
→ Basic play
→ Target play

Training unit:
→ Warm-up
→ Basic exercise
→ Basic play
→ Target play

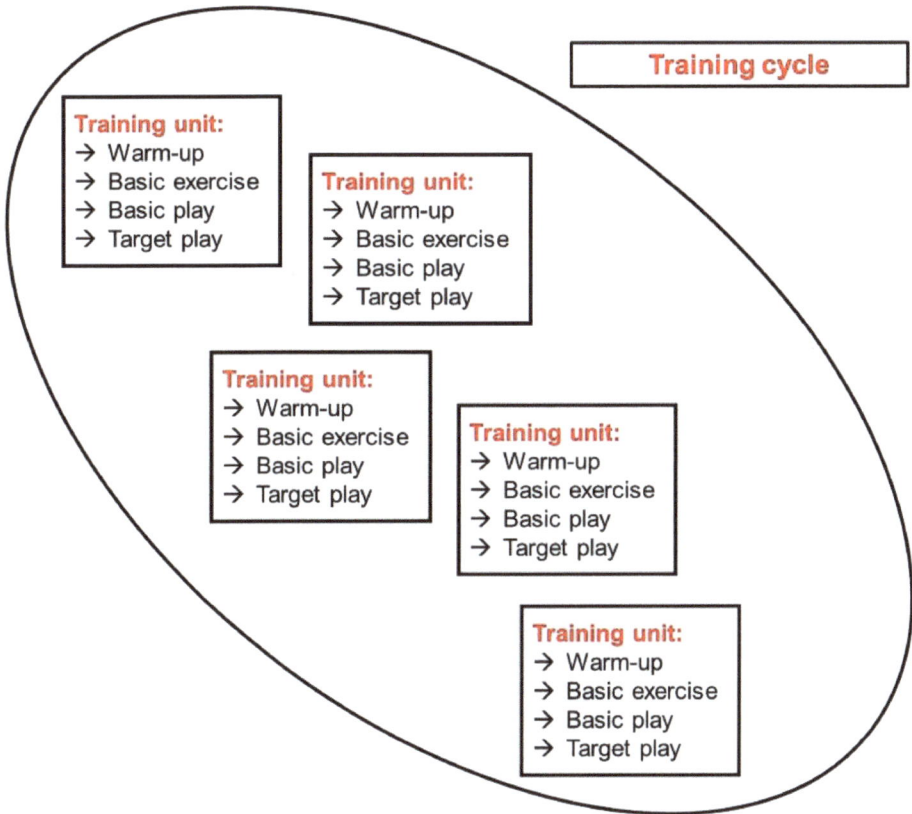

Creating well-structured training units

A clear structure is important for the annual schedule as well as for the planning of the individual training units.

- Work with parts (see monthly schedule). You should work on a special topic over a certain period of time, especially in the training of youth teams. That way, you can repeat exercises and make sure the players memorize the courses.
- Each training unit should have a clear training focus. Do not mix topics within a training unit, but make sure that each exercise has a well-defined objective.
- The players are corrected in accordance with the training unit's focus (when training the defense, defense actions are corrected and pointed out).

In each individual planning phase, training units that focus on improving speed of play will play a role in one way or another. Completely new fast break concepts should be developed during the preparatory phase already, whereas decision-making processes, free play, and adjusting from defense to offense play may be improved continuously during all phases.

2. Structuring a training unit

The focus of the training should run like a red thread through the entire unit. It is advisable to follow the basic timescale below:
- Approx. 10 (15) minutes – warm-up.
- Approx. 20 (30) minutes – basic exercises (2 to 3 exercises max. plus goalkeeper warm-up shooting).
- Approx. 20 (30) minutes – basic play.
- Approx. 10 (15) minutes – target play.

1st timescale for a 60-minute training unit / 2nd timescale in brackets for a 90-minute training unit.

Warm-up practices
- Opening of the training unit: It may be advisable to start the training unit with a ritual (get together in a circle, exchanging high-fives) and to explain the contents and the objectives of the training unit to the players.
- Basic warm-up (jogging, activation of blood circulation and the musculoskeletal system).
- Stretching/strengthening/mobilization (preparing the body for the physical stress of the training unit).
- Short games (these should already focus on the objective of the training unit).

Basic exercises
- Ball familiarization (focused on the objective of the training unit).
- Goalkeeper warm-up shooting (focused on the objective of the training unit).
- Individual technique and tactics training.
- Technique and tactics training in small groups.

In general, the running and passing paths are predefined during the basic exercises (you may increase and vary the requirements during the course of the exercise).

Additional information on basic exercise
- Each player should do the drill (switch quickly).
- Very frequent repetitions.
- The players should rotate or do the drill on both sides simultaneously / slightly delayed to avoid long waiting periods.
- Practice individually (1-on-1 to 2-on-2 max.).
- Add additional tasks/drills, if applicable (to make the exercise more complex).

Basic play

Most of all, the basic play differs from the basic exercise in such a way that now there are several **options for action** (decisions). The player(s) should realize the respective options and make the ideal decision. Here, the players practice decision-making in particular.

- The players should now implement what they practiced during the basic exercises under **competitive conditions**.
- Working with alternative actions – practicing the decision-making process.
- The players should repeat the drill frequently and try out different actions.
- Working in small groups (3-on-3 to 4-on-4 max.).

Target play

- The players now implement what they practiced before in free play. To increase their motivation, you may award additional points or additional attacks for correct implementation.
- In the target play, the players implement what they practiced before (5-on-5, 6-on-6).

Depending on the contents and the objectives of the training unit, you may have to slightly adjust the timescales of the basic exercise and basic play.

Set topics

- Individual training of the players according to the respective conceptual training framework (DHB or the club's individual conceptual framework).
- Tactical training of defense and offense systems (age-dependent):
    - From man coverage to a 6-0 defense system, for example.
    - From 1-on1 to 6-on-6 with initial actions practiced in teams, for example.

Choose topic of training unit:

→ Red thread

Warm up:
Time:
- approx. 10 (15) minutes

Practices:
- "Playful warm-up"
- Games
- Coordination runs
- (Stretching and strengthening)

Basic exercise:
Time:
- approx. 20 (30) minutes

Characteristics:
- Individual/Small groups

Practices:
- Exact instructions re. course of the exercise
- Variants with exact instructions re. the course
- From simple to complex
- No waiting periods for players

Basic play:
Time:
- approx. 20 (30) minutes

Characteristics:
- Small groups

Practices:
- Exact instructions re. course
- Competition

Target play:
Time:
- approx. 10 (15) minutes

Characteristics:
- Team play (small groups)

Practices:
- Free play with the contents of the basic exercise and basic play
- Competition

3. Roles/tasks of the coach

It is mainly the personality and the behavior of the coach that makes the training a success. Therefore, it is important to observe certain behavioral rules to guarantee a successful training. The coach's social skills have an impact as important as his expertise.

A coach should:
- describe the training and its objectives to his team at the beginning of the training unit
- always speak loud and clear
- talk from such a position that all players can hear his instructions and corrections
- recognize and correct mistakes and give advice when correcting
- mainly correct what is part of the training objective
- point out and compliment on individual progress (give the player self-confidence)
- support and permanently challenge the players
- always be a role model - during training and games, but also outside the court
- come to training and games well-prepared and in a timely manner

4. Training units

No.: 1	Improving passing precision when initiating the first wave		★★	90

Opening part		Main part			
X	Warm-up/Stretching		Offense/Individual		Jumping power
	Running exercise	X	Offense/Small groups		Sprint contest
X	Short game		Offense/Team		Goalkeeper
	Coordination	X	Offense/Series of shots		**Final part**
	Coordination run		Defense/Individual		
	Strengthening		Defense/Small groups		Closing game
X	Ball familiarization		Defense/Team		Final sprint
X	Goalkeeper warm-up shooting		Athletics		
			Endurance		

Key:

✖   Cone

△1   Attacking player

●1   Defense player

▭   Small gym mat

◼   Ball box

Equipment required:

➜ 4 small gym mats, 8 cones, ball box with sufficient number of handballs

Description:

The objective of this training unit is to improve running paths, passing and the decision-making process during the first wave. After a warm-up running exercise, the subsequent short game already includes quick adjustment exercises and long passes. During the ball familiarization phase and the goalkeeper warm-up shooting, the players practice playing long passes before they combine several actions with first wave initiation in a series of shots. The closing small group exercises finally focus on making passing decisions.

The training unit consists of the following key exercises:
- Warm-up/Stretching (individual exercise: 10 minutes/total time: 10 minutes)
- Short game (15/25)
- Ball familiarization (10/35)
- Goalkeeper warm-up shooting (10/45)
- Offense/Series of shots (15/60)
- Offense/Small groups (15/75)
- Offense/Small groups (15/90)

Training unit total time: 90 minutes

No.: 1-1	Warm-up/Stretching	10	10

Course:

- The players make pairs.
- One player per team has a ball.
- The players without a ball crisscross outside of the 9-meter zone in the bottom half of the court and do different running moves (hopping, sidestepping...) (A).
- The players with a ball dribble through the 9-meter zone in the bottom half of the court and do different running moves while performing different dribbling variants (dribbling with the non-/throwing hand, alternately while hopping, sidestepping...) (B).
- Once the coach whistles, the players without a ball run into the other half of the court (C).
- The players with a ball try to get into a good passing position (dribbling the ball one time, if necessary) (D) and pass the ball to their teammate (E).
- Afterwards, all players run into the other half of the court and start the course over with switched tasks.
- The players should increase the passing distance during the further course of the exercise.

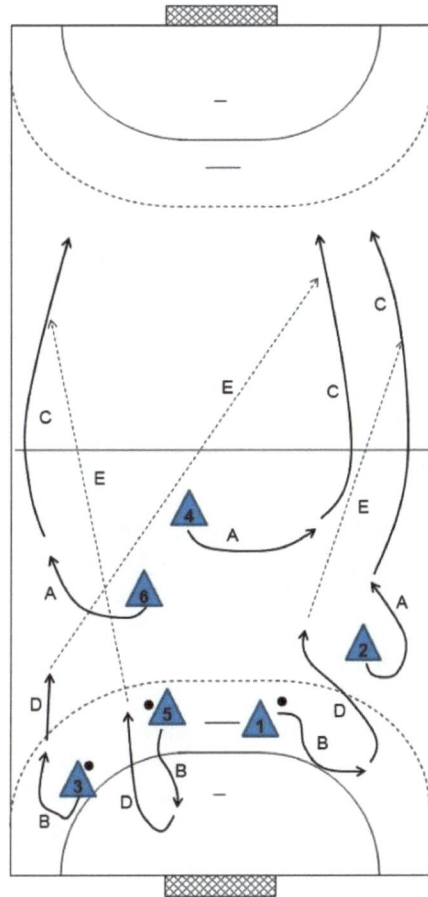

| No.: 1-2 | Short game | 15 | 25 |

Setting:
- Position four mats as shown in the figure.

Course:
- Each team defends two mats in the same half of the court.
- In the beginning, the team in ball possession tries to lay down the ball on one of their opponents' mats as often as possible (C) by playing passes cleverly (A and B).
- Every time the players manage to lay down the ball, they get a point.
- Once the ball lies on the mat, the players of both teams may try to secure it (D), except for the player who has laid it down.
- If the previous attacking team wins the ball again, they play on the other mat in the same half of the court.
- If the previous defending team wins the ball, the teams change the half of the court (E and F). Now the players have to lay down the ball on one of the mats in the other half (G and H).
- Which team scores highest?

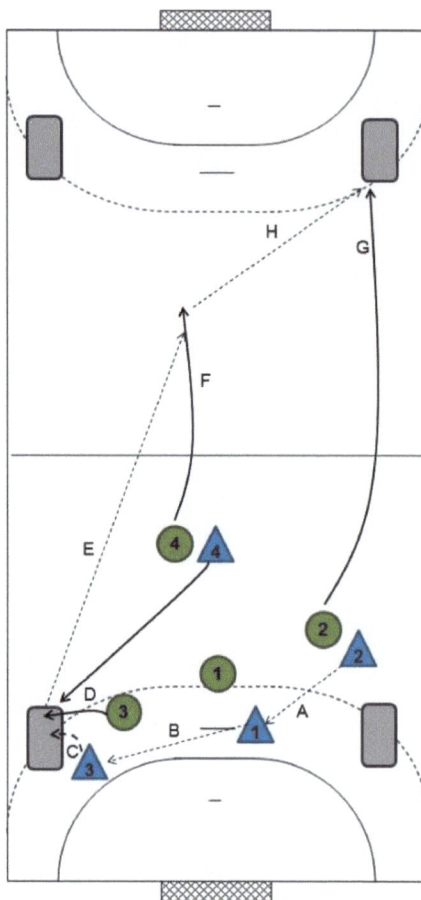

⚠ The players should immediately try to secure the ball once it has been laid down on the mat.

⚠ The players should quickly recognize which team is in ball possession and play on the respective mat.

No.: 1-3	Ball familiarization	10	35

Setting:

- Define the starting positions with cones (see figure).
- Make groups of five players each.

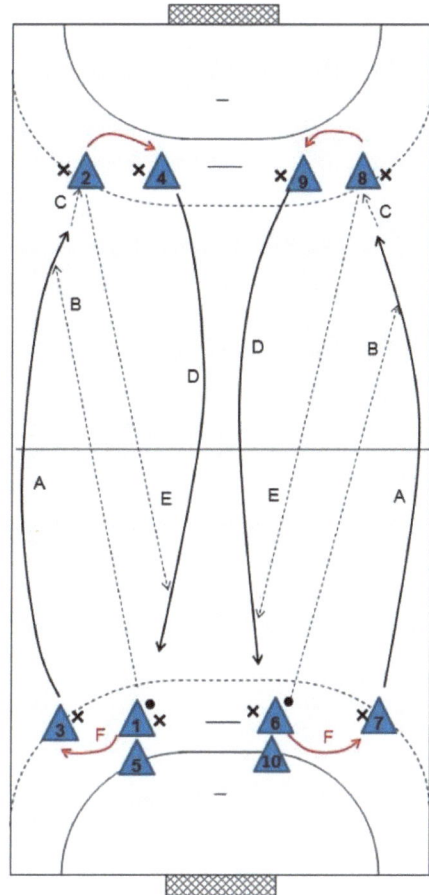

Course:

- 3 starts to run a fast break without a ball towards the other side (A) and receives a pass from 1 into his running path (B).

- 3 passes to 2 (C) and the course starts over on the other side.

- 4 starts to run a fast break without a ball (D) and receives a pass from 2 into his running path (E).

- 4 passes to 5, and so on.

- After the pass, 1 and 2 move to the other cone (F) and become the next running players.

- The other groups do the course in parallel.

Competition:

- The groups do the course in parallel. The players who have passed the ball 20 times in a row first without losing it get a point.
- If a group loses the ball, they start over counting from 1.

⚠ The players should run a curve so that they can catch the ball in an optimal way.

⚠ The players should run to the other side at high speed.

No.: 1-4	Goalkeeper warm-up shooting	10	45

Course:

- ▲1 starts from the corner, without a ball (A), and receives a pass from ▲G1 into his running path (B).

- As soon as ▲G1 has passed the ball, ▲2 starts from the other corner, without a ball (C), and also receives a pass from ▲G1 into his running path (D).

- The other players do the same course subsequently.

- The players who received a pass, line up in the center (E and F) and start a series of shots for ▲G2 as instructed (hands, top, bottom) (G and H), as soon as all players have arrived.

- Afterwards, the players change sides, ▲G2 passes the ball and ▲G1 gets the series of shots.

⚠ The players first have to line up in the center in order to create a proper series of shots for ▲G2.

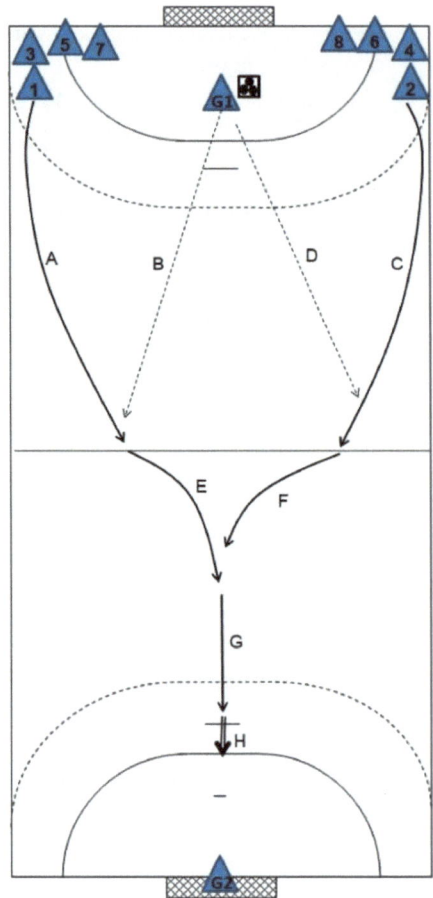

No.: 1-5	Offense/Series of shots	15	60

Course:

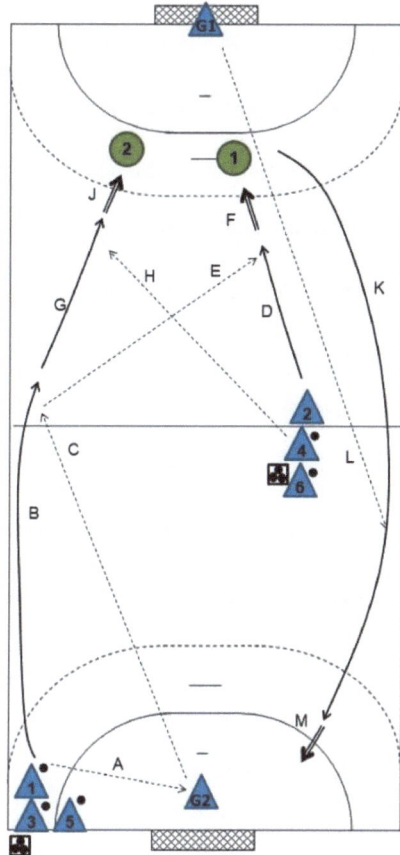

- 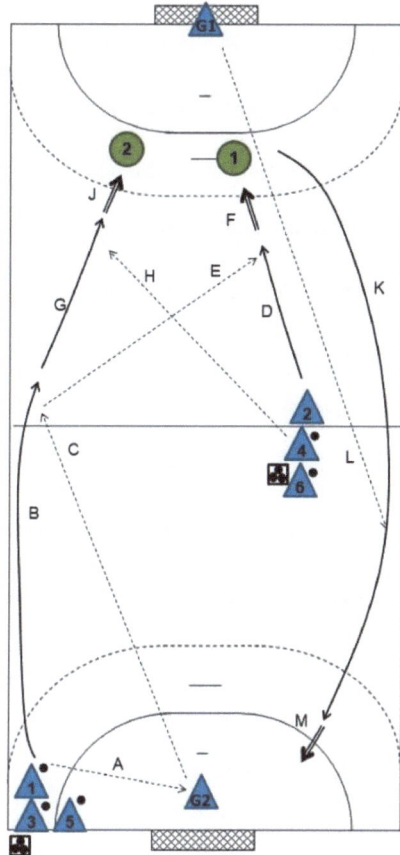 passes the ball to the goalkeeper (A), starts running a fast break (B), and receives the ball from 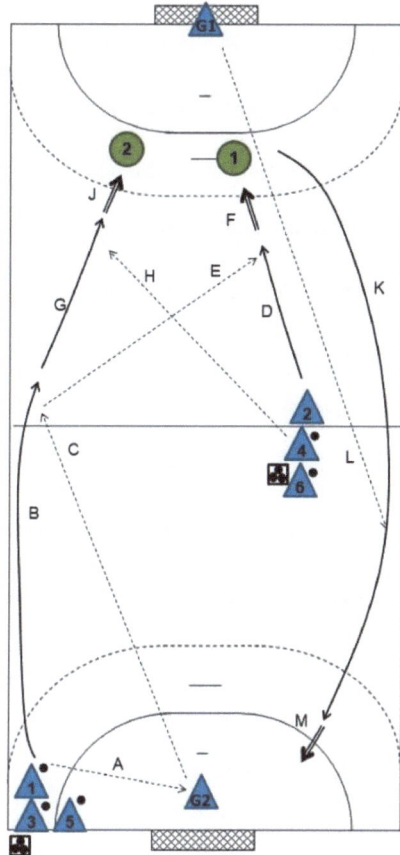 (C).

- 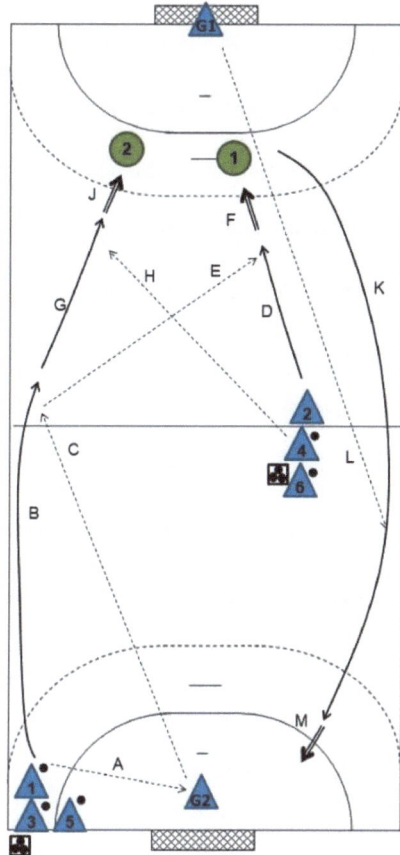 starts from the center line (D), receives a pass from 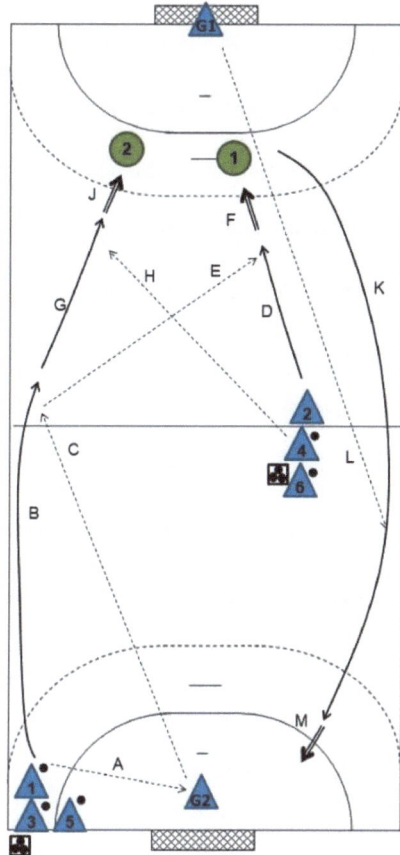 into his running path (E), and shoots over 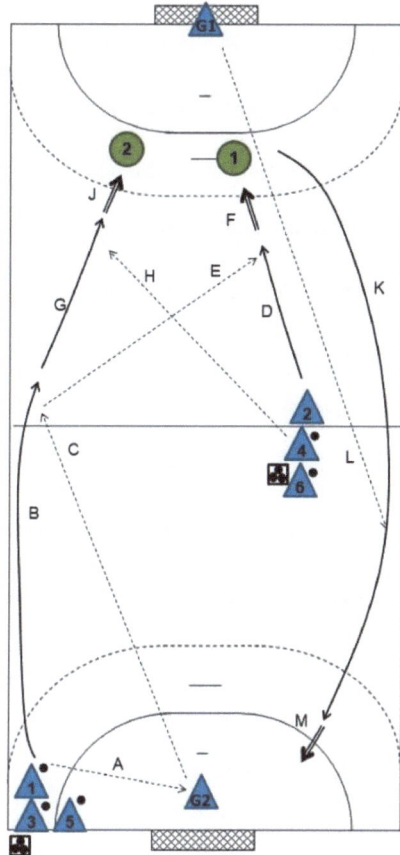 who serves as defensive block (F).

- After playing the pass, 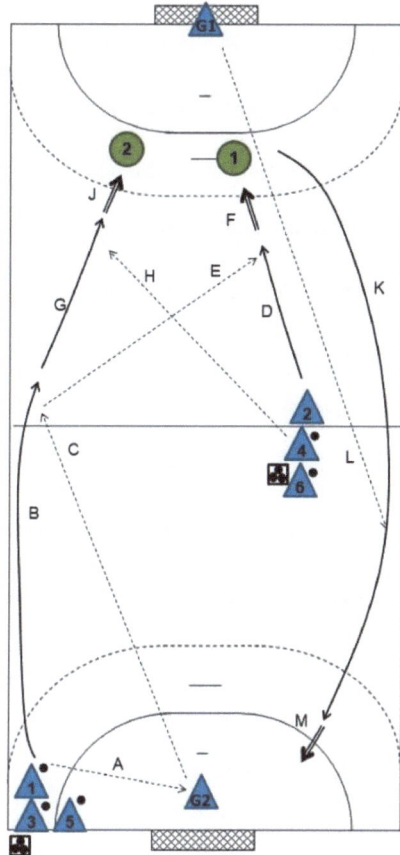 has slowed down, but now speeds up again (G), receives a pass from 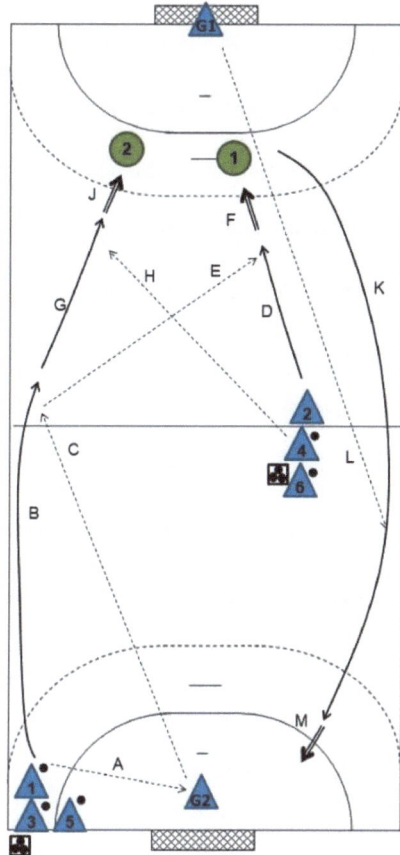 into his running path (H), and shoots over 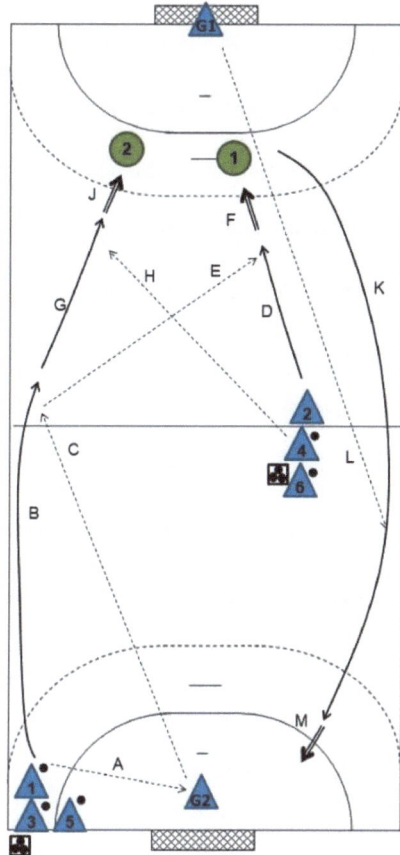, who also serves as defensive block (J).

- During the shot of 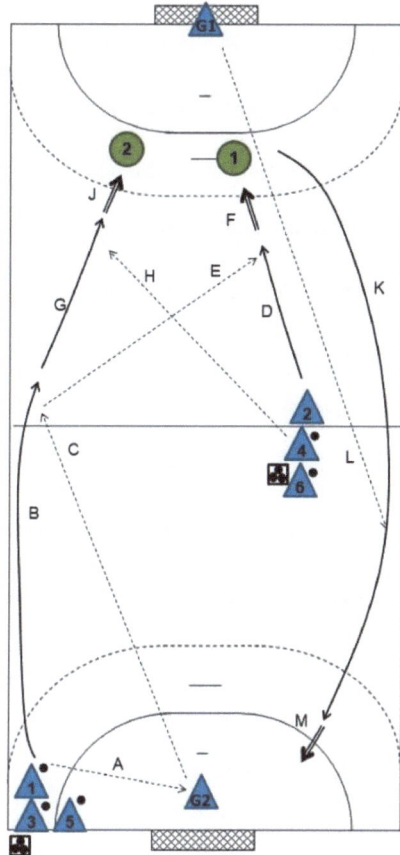 (J), 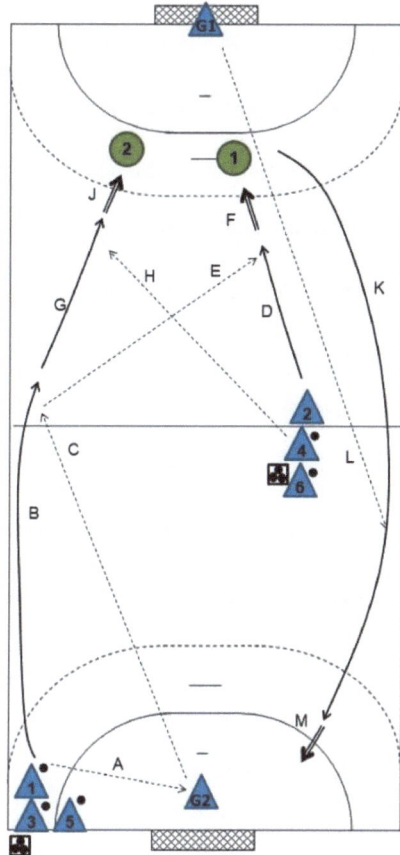 starts running a fast break (K).

- 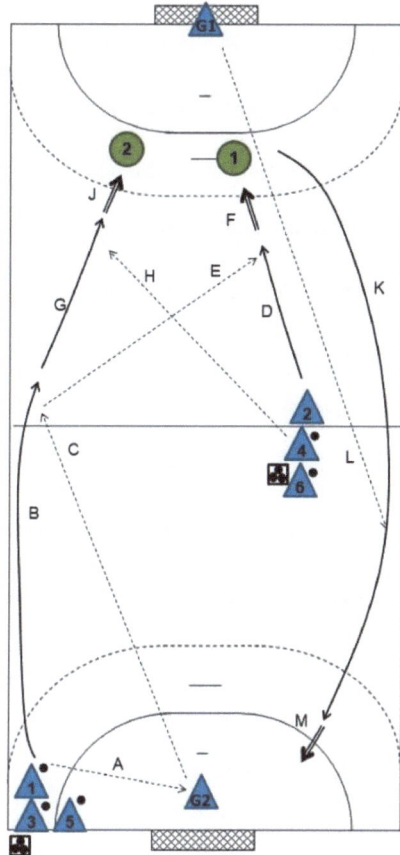 secures the ball and passes it into the running path of 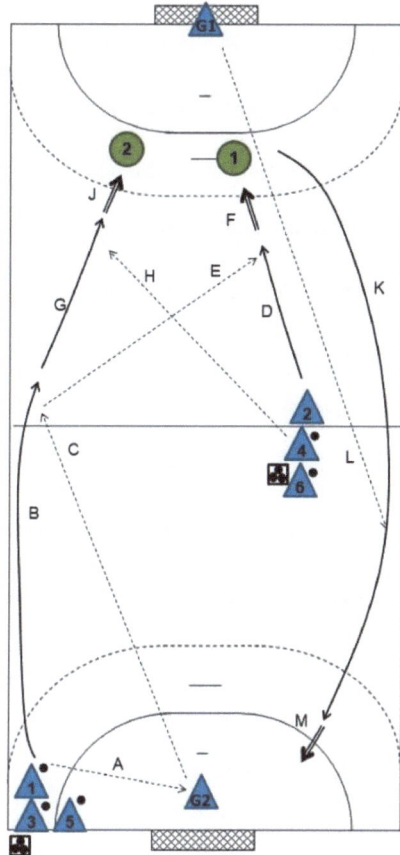 (L). 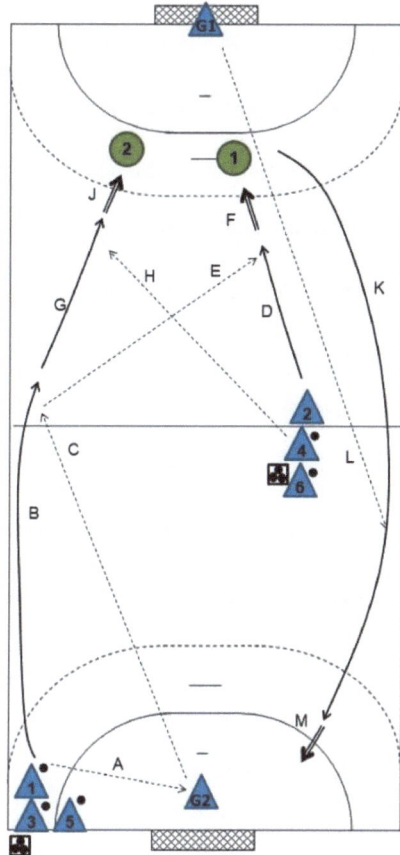 eventually shoots at the goal (M).

- After serving as defensive block, 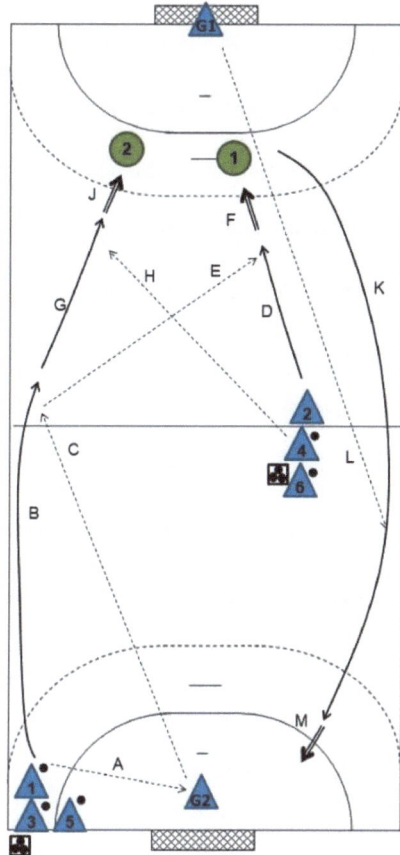 takes over the position of 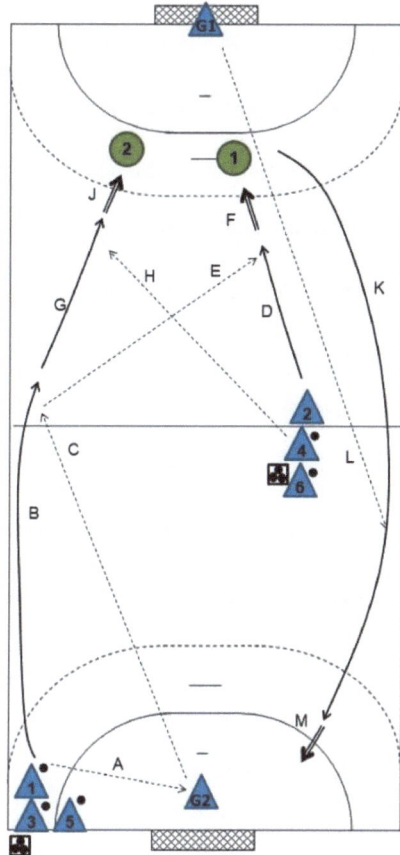,

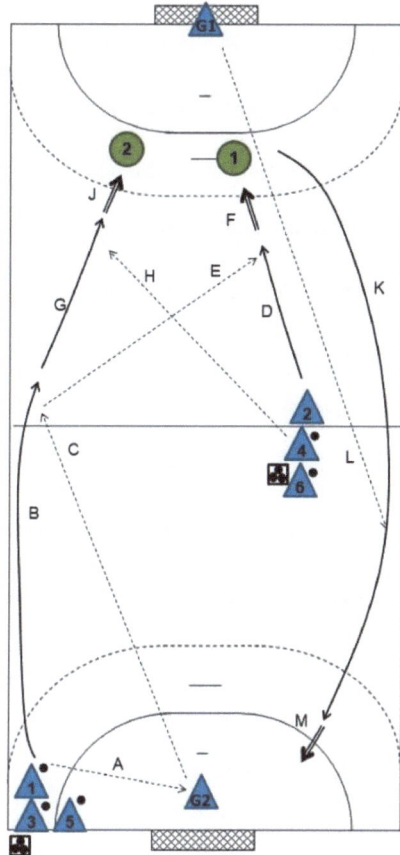 becomes the new block player and takes over the position of 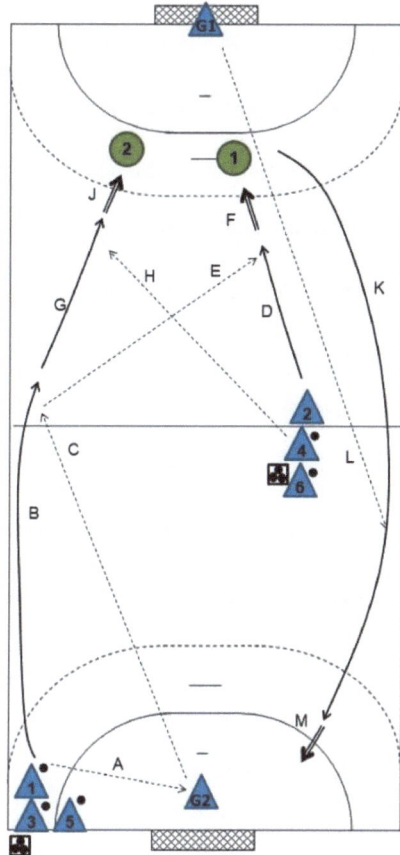, 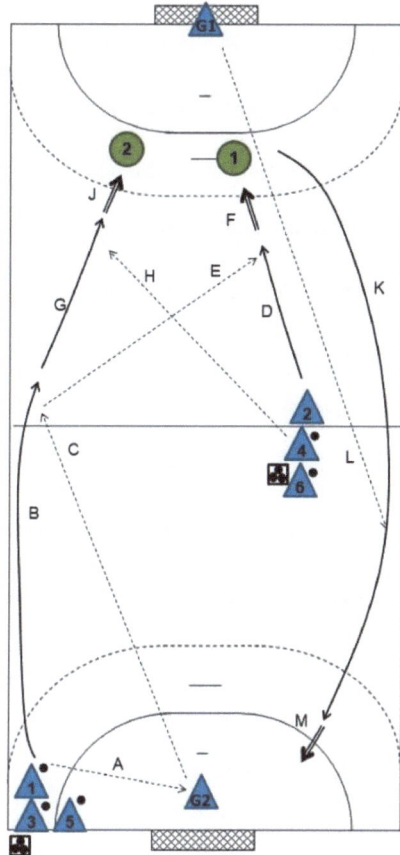 lines up behind 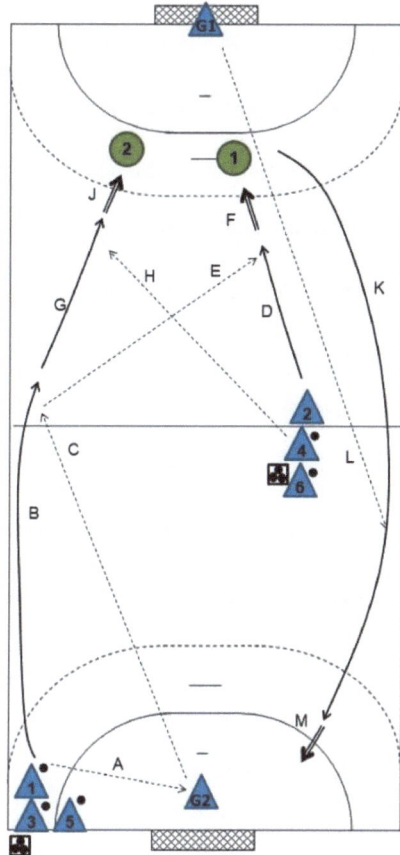 with a ball, and 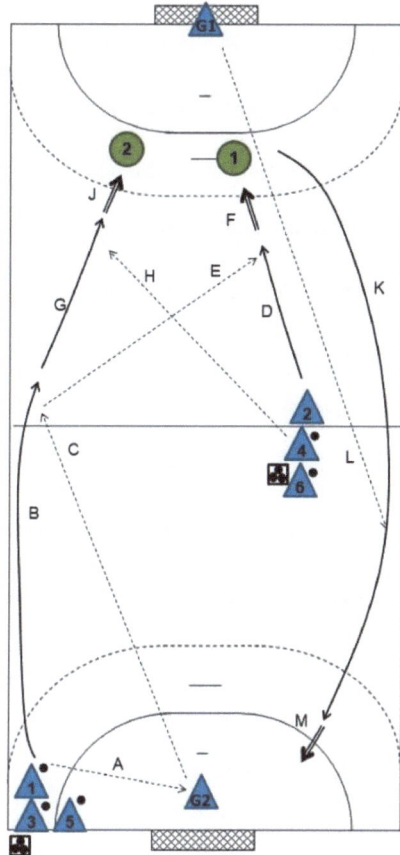 lines up behind 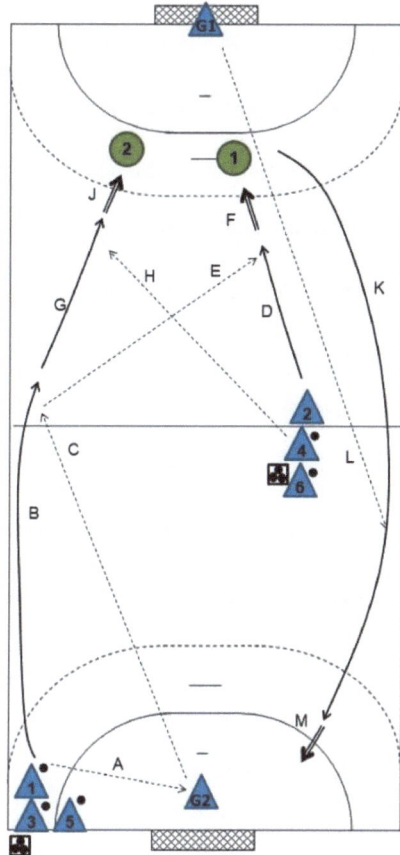 with a ball.

- Afterwards, the players repeat the course.

Variant:

- The players must play 1-on-1 against 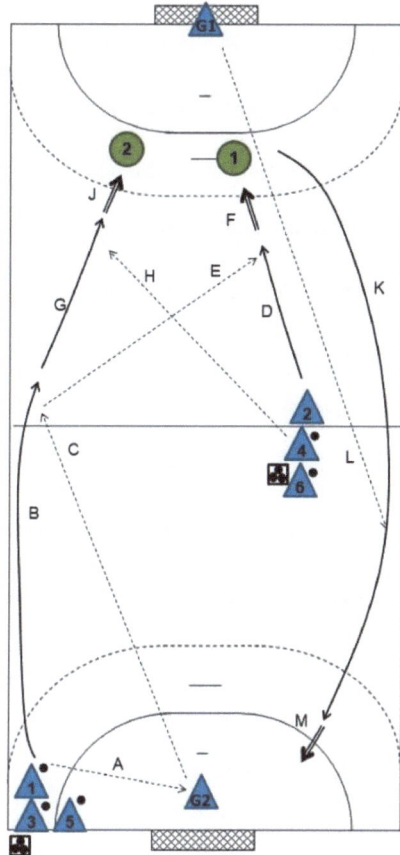 instead of shooting over a defensive block.

⚠ The players should run a curve during their fast break so that they can catch the ball in an optimal way.

⚠ The defensive block players should start their fast break immediately during the second shot.

⚠ Change the side after a while.

No.: 1-6	Offense/Small groups	15	75

Setting:

- Define the running path with a cone.

Course:

- 🔺2, 🔺3, and the defense players 🔵1 and 🔵2 initially sit on the floor at the center line.
- 🔺1 passes the ball to 🟢G2 (A), starts running a fast break (B), and receives the ball from the goalkeeper (C).
- 🔺1 keeps running, passes the ball to 🟢G1 (D), runs around the cone, starts approaching the other side (E), and receives the ball from 🟢G1 into his running path (F).
- As soon as 🟢G1 (F) plays the return pass, 🔺2, 🔺3, 🔵1, and 🔵2 get up and enter the game.
- 🔺1, 🔺2, and 🔺3 now play 3-on-2 (G, J, K, and L) against 🔵1 and 🔵2 (H) until one of the attacking players has shot at the goal.
- The shooting player lines up behind 🔺5 with a ball, the other two attacking players and the defense players go back to the center line.
- Now, the players start the next round.

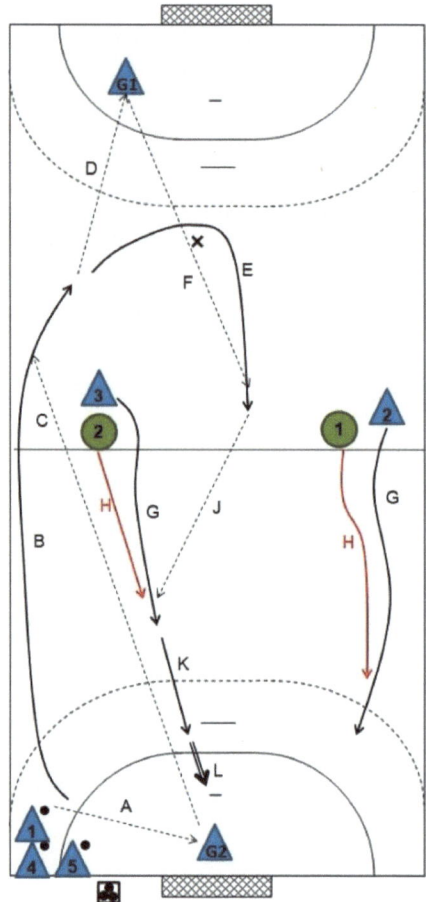

⚠ Change the defense players and the goalkeeper after a while, and let the players do the course on the other side as well.

No.: 1-7	Offense/Small groups	15	90

Setting:
- Divide the court in two longitudinal halves with cones.

Course:
- 1 and 2, and 5 and 6 (on the other side, in opposite direction) run to the other half of the playing field at a relaxed pace (A) and pass a ball in pairs (B).
- Once they have arrived on the other side, they pass the ball to the goalkeeper (C).
- Now, the subsequent action starts.

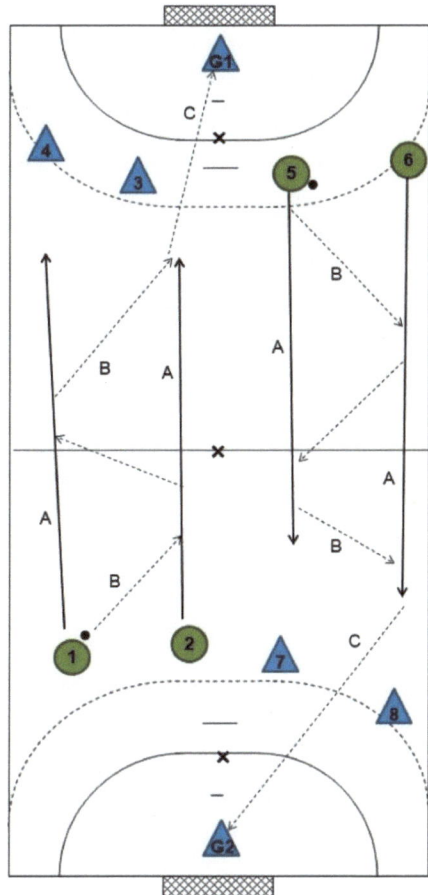

- 3 and 4 run a fast break, playing 2-on-2 (D and G) against 1 and 2 (E), 7 and 8 run and play in the opposite direction (J, K, L, M, and N) against 5 and 6 (E).
- The goalkeepers decide whether to play a long pass (F) or a short pass (H) as the initial action.
- The teams of 2 change the sides and tasks for the next round.
- Which team has scored highest after 10 attacks, for example?

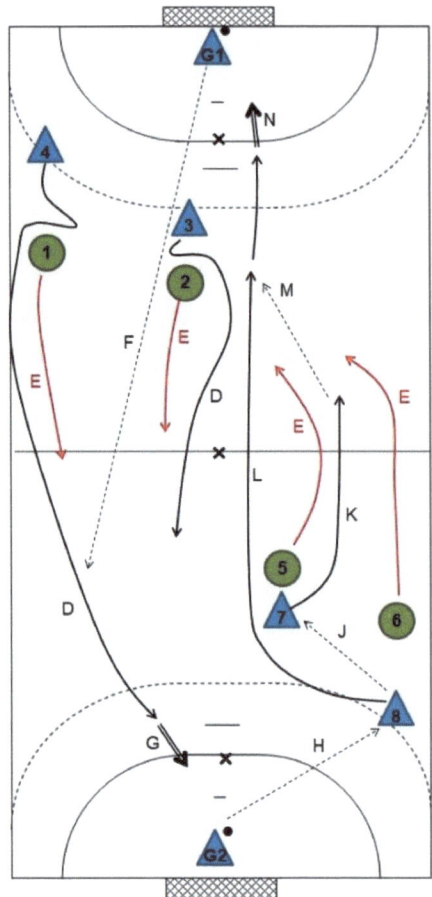

Notes:

_____

_____

_____

_____

_____

_____

No.: 2	Quick adjustment to a fast break after a defense action		★★★	90

Opening part		Main part			
X	Warm-up/Stretching		Offense/Individual		Jumping power
	Running exercise		Offense/Small groups		Sprint contest
	Short game		Offense/Team		Goalkeeper
	Coordination		Offense/Series of shots		
X	Coordination run		Defense/Individual		**Final part**
	Strengthening	X	Defense/Small groups		Closing game
X	Ball familiarization	X	Defense/Team	X	Final sprint
X	Goalkeeper warm-up shooting		Athletics		
			Endurance		

Key:

✗ Cone

△1 Attacking player

◯1 Defense player

▬ Small gym mat

⬛ Ball box

▦ Hurdle

◯ Hoop

Bibs in different colors

Equipment required:
- 6 small gym mats, 5 hurdles, 12 hoops, 4 cones, 2 ball boxes with sufficient number of handballs, 2 × 3 bibs in two different colors, whistle

Description:

The objective of this training unit is to practice the quick adjustment from defense play to fast break initiation. Following the warm-up phase with a coordination run exercise and the ball familiarization phase, the goalkeeper warm-up shooting combines a preparatory defense exercise and a series of shots for the goalkeeper. During the two subsequent defense exercises, the players practice quick adjustment from defense work to fast break countermovement. A 4-on-4 game and a sprint contest complete this training unit.

The training unit consists of the following key exercises:
- Warm-up/Stretching (individual exercise: 10 minutes/total time: 10 minutes)
- Coordination run (10/20)
- Ball familiarization (10/30)
- Goalkeeper warm-up shooting (10/40)
- Defense/Small groups (10/50)
- Defense/Small groups (15/65)
- Defense/Team (15/80)
- Closing sprint (10/90)

Total training time: 90 minutes

No.: 2-1	Warm-up/Stretching	10	10

Course:

- Two players each crisscross the 9-meter zone together while passing a ball.
- As soon as the coach whistles, the teams of 2 start running a fast break to the opposite 9-meter zone. While doing this, they should keep passing the ball, without dribbling it however.
- Afterwards, the players start the course over in the other 9-meter zone.

Variants:

- Jump shot passes.
- The team of 2 which is last must do 10 quick jumping jacks, for example.
- The teams may try to steal each other's ball. All teams that arrive the 9-meter zone without a ball must do 10 quick jumping jacks, for example.

The players perform stretching exercises together.

No.: 2-2	Coordination run	10	20

Setting:

- Position the hurdles and hoops as shown in the figure.
- Put some gym mats on the floor for the push-ups/sit-ups, if necessary.

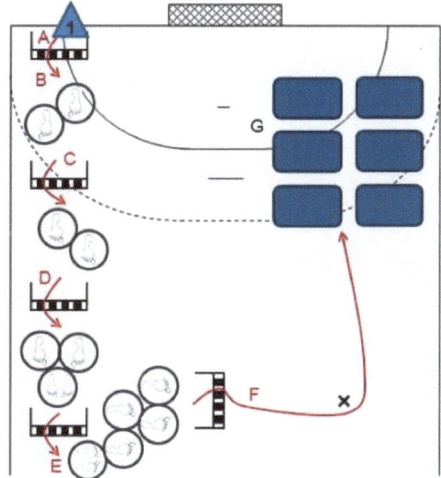

Course:

- 1 stands in the initial position, right in front of the first hurdle.
- On command, 1 jumps over the hurdle with both feet and should also land with both feet on the floor (A and B). Afterwards, 1 jumps through the two hoops with his left foot and lands in front of the second hurdle with both feet on the floor again (C).
- 1 jumps over the hurdle with both feet and should also land with both feet on the floor. Afterwards, 1 jumps through the two hoops with his right foot and lands with both feet on the floor right in front of the third hurdle (D).
- 1 jumps over the hurdle with both feet and should also land with both feet on the floor. Afterwards, 1 jumps though the next hoops and over the next hurdles, as shown in the figure.
- After the fourth hurdle, 1 takes a 90° turn and keeps on jumping (E).
- After the last hurdle, 1 immediately sprints to the cone (F) and to the gym mats.
- On one of the gym mats, 1 does 10 push-ups and 10 sit-ups.

Overall course:

- The players do the course twice at 70% speed. Afterwards, they immediately start the third and fourth round, at 100% speed however.

⚠ The players should jump over the hurdles and through the hoops quickly and without an additional jump (also when taking the 90° turn) (E).

No.: 2-3	Ball familiarization	10	30

Setting:

- The players stand pairwise, as shown in the figure, with each pair having one handball.

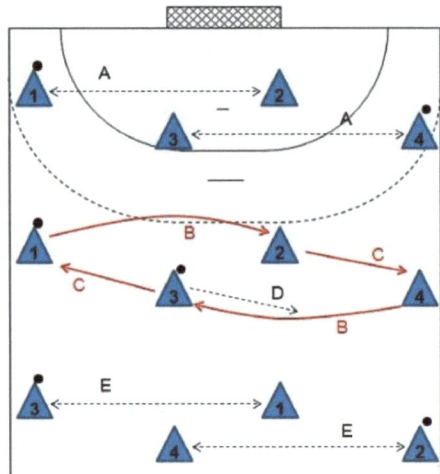

Course:

- ▲1 and ▲2 keep passing the ball while moving back and forth; so do ▲3 and ▲4 (A).
- On the coach's command, the players on the outer court (▲1 and ▲4) start to dynamically run forward and dribble to the other side (B). If the players on the outer side do not have the ball at that time, they first must receive a pass before the running move (D).
- ▲2 and ▲3 immediately take over the positions from ▲1 and ▲4 clockwise (C).
- Afterwards, the players start passing the ball again (E).

⚠ ▲1 and ▲4 must take a 180° turn after the running move and before the first pass (E).

No.: 2-4	Goalkeeper warm-up shooting	10	40

Setting:

- Position three cones right in front of the center line as shown in the figure.
- Provide a ball box with a sufficient number of handballs

Course:

- The attacking players (1, 2, and 3) start on command and try to touch the cone behind the defense line (C) playing 1-on-1 against the defense players (1, 2, and 3).
- The defense players try to prevent the attacking players from touching the cone (A and B).
- All players do the drill in a highly dynamic manner.
- Once C whistles (D), the players start the subsequent action:
  - o 1, 2, and 3 immediately run towards the 7-meter line, receiving a pass from 1, 2, and 3 (E).
  - o As soon as the three players each have a ball and are ready, they start a series of shots for G (F).
  - o 1 shoots top left, 2 shoots top right, and 3 shoots bottom left.
  - o G saves the two balls shot at the top of the goal and makes a hurdle jump in order to save the ball shot at the bottom of the goal.
- Afterwards, 1 becomes a defense player, 1 becomes the new attacking player (G), 1 lines up with a ball. Now the next round starts.
- This time, the first shot must be top right, and G makes a hurdle jump in order to save the third shot at the bottom right corner, etc.

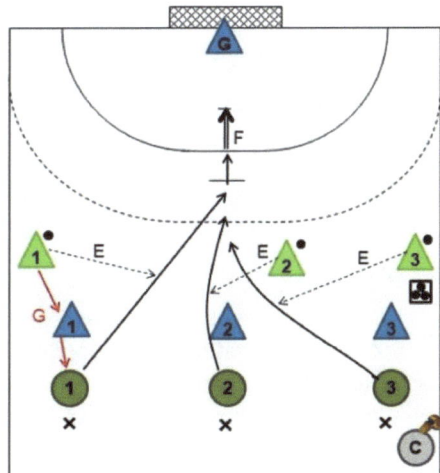

When is the right time for Ⓒ to whistle?
- As soon as one of the three defense players has managed to tackle an attacking player for 2 seconds.
- As soon as one of the three attacking players has managed to touch the respective cone.
- If it takes too long.

⚠ The defense players should start a countermovement and get in a good passing position (E) as soon as the coach has whistled.

No.: 2-5	Defense/Small groups	10	50

Setting:
- Position two cone goals as shown in the figure.

Course:
- 🔺1 and 🔺2 play 2-on-2 against 🟢1 and 🟢2. Their aim is to run through the cone goal with the ball (A and B).
- If they succeed, the players immediately switch tasks; 🟢1 and 🟢2 start the countermovement, receive a pass from Ⓒ (D), and also play 2-on-2 on the other side, against 🔺1 and 🔺2.
- 🟢1 and 🟢2 become defense players and wait until 🔺1 and 🔺2 approach the cone goal as attacking players during the subsequent action.
- The players repeat the course until each team of 2 has played offense and defense four times. The players should count the successful defense actions themselves.
- If the 2-on-2 game lasts too long, Ⓒ whistles (C). This also is the sign for the defense players to start the countermovement (D).
- Afterwards, each player must do e.g. 10 push-ups for each unsuccessful defense action (max. 40 push-ups).

Overall course:
- If there are enough players, let them do the course in two groups in parallel.
- Make new teams for the second round.

⚠️ The defense players should start the countermovement in a highly dynamic manner.

⚠️ The defense players should work together as a team and keep communicating during the exercise.

No.: 2-6	Defense/Small groups	15	65

Setting:
- Define a defense corridor with two cones as shown in the figure.
- Position one cone a few meters behind the center line.

Course for the attacking players:
- 1, 2, and 3 play 3-on-3 against 1, 2, and 3.
- The three attacking players should challenge the defense players by initiating 1-on-1 actions (B) or crossing moves (C).

Course for the defense players:
- The defense players should act as a team when defending against the attacking players' actions and more or less stand on one line (D).

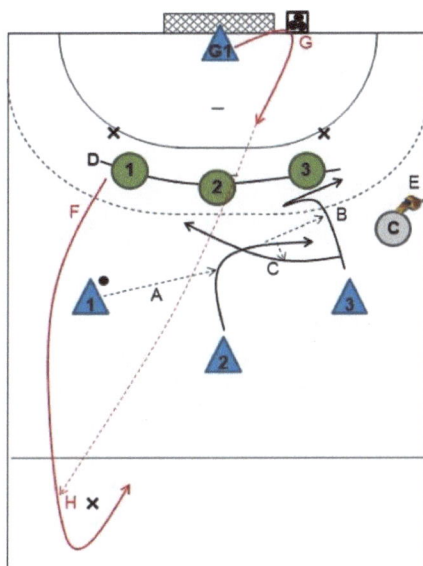

The defense players' subsequent action starts according to the following criteria:
- The defense players have won the ball.
- The attacking players have scored a goal.
- c whistles (E):
  - o In case of a foul.
  - o Anytime during the attack.

Subsequent action:

- The outmost defense player (1)
immediately starts to run a fast
break (F).
- G1 either picks up the ball shot at
the goal or a ball from the ball box
provided (G) and passes it into
the fast break path of 1 , as soon
as he is about to cross the center
line (H).
- 1 makes a jump shot at the
goal, over the defensive block (
2 and 3) (J). 1 , 2 , and 3
should refrain from intervening.
- As soon as the action is over, the
players move to the next position.

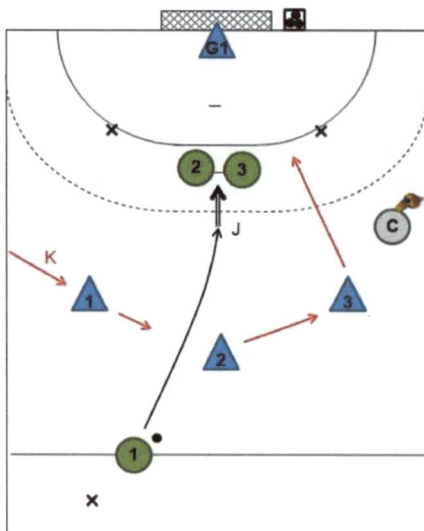

3 becomes the new defense player and a new attacking player enters the
game.

Overall course:
- The players each do the course (playing on each position once) one to two
times (depending on the total number of players). For each goal the
attacking players score as long as a given player plays defense (three
attacks), the respective defense player must do 10 push-ups, for example.
- The waiting players (for a larger number of players) should do a coordination
exercise at the sideline (juggling with tennis balls, for example).

⚠ The defense player who is next to start the fast break should carefully watch
out for his starting sign and start the countermovement IMMEDIATELY and at top
speed.

⚠ G1 must pass the ball into the fast break path of 1 as fast as he can (H), so
that 1 is able to run without slowing down and to eventually shoot at the goal (J).

⚠ 1 shoots at the goal as soon as he has arrived the 7-meter line at the latest
(J). 2 and 3 should work together with G1 and serve as defensive block.

No.: 2-7	Defense/Team	15	80

Setting:

- Make two to three teams. The teams play 4-on-4 against each other.
- Define a shooting corridor on each side of the playing field with two cones.
- Put a ball box next to each goal.

Course:

- The defense players must defend in front of the 9-meter line.
- The attacking players may enter the 9-meter zone for a goal shot only; they must not enter the zone behind the defense line without a ball (G).
- The attacking players should try to get into a good shooting position through 1-on-1 actions or team interactions, e.g. crossing moves (B).
- If the defense players have won the ball or one of the attacking players has shot at the goal, the defense players start a countermovement at once (D). G either picks up the ball shot at the goal or a new ball from the ball box provided (E) and passes it as fast as he can (F).
- There is no throw-off at the center line.

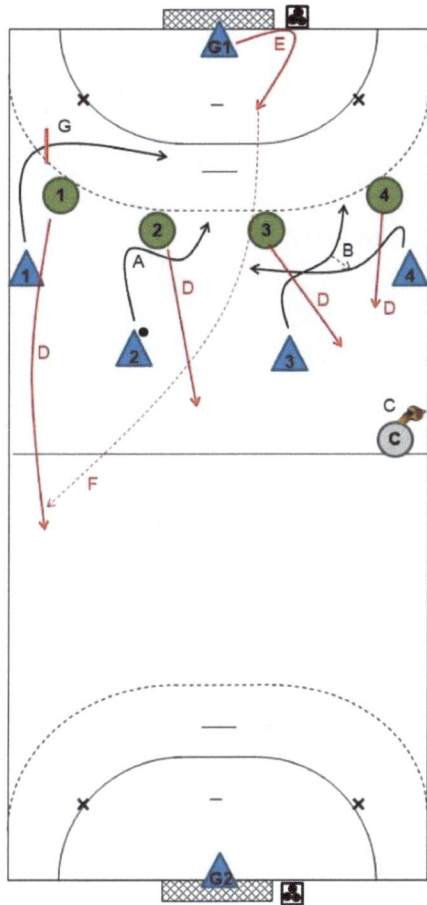

The subsequent action also starts, if

- Ⓒ whistles two times. If an attack lasts too long, Ⓒ should whistle any time during the attack (C). This is the sign for the defense players to immediately start the countermovement (D).

Overall course:

- Playing time is four minutes each. If there are three teams, the teams play against each of the other teams. If there are two teams only, make new teams.
- The players should count the goals of their team themselves. For each goal against, the players must do three push-ups in the end, for example.

⚠ The defense players should defend against the attacking players' actions in a highly dynamic manner, move along with them and communicate permanently.

⚠ The defense players should carefully pay attention and watch out for the end of the attack or the two whistle blows of ©, and then start the countermovement at once.

No.: 2-8	Final sprint		10	90

Setting:

- Put nine hoops on the floor as shown in the figure.
- Make teams of two players each.

Course:

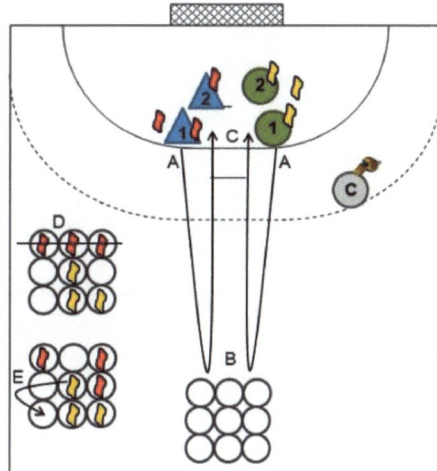

- Two teams play against each other.
- Each team gets three bibs of the same color.
- On command, ▲1 and ●1 each start to sprint while holding a bib in their hand (A), put the bib in one of the hoops (B), and sprint back (C).
- Afterwards, ▲2 and ●2 start, also put their bib in one of the empty hoops, and sprint back.
- Then it is the turn of ▲1 and ●1 again who put the last bib in an empty hoop.
- If a team manages to mark a line of 3 (horizontal (D), vertical, or diagonal), this team wins the game at once.
- If none of the teams has managed to mark a line of 3, ▲1 and ●1 sprint back again and exchange a high five with ▲2 and ●2, respectively.
- ▲2 and ●2 run to the hoops again, pick up a bib of their team's color and put it into another empty hoop (E). If one of the teams now has managed to mark a line of 3, this team has won the game. If still no team was successful, the players run back and it is the turn of ▲1 and ●1 again. The players repeat the course until one of the teams has managed to mark a line of 3.
- Afterwards, it's the next two teams' turn.

⚠ There is only one bib per hoop allowed.

⚠ After starting to sprint, the players have no more than five seconds to put the bib into one of the hoops (calculation: three seconds to sprint to the cones and two seconds to put the bib into a hoop).

No.: 3	Improving speed play for fast break situations	★★★	90

Opening part		Main part			
X	Warm-up/Stretching		Offense/Individual		Jumping power
	Running exercise	X	Offense/Small groups		Sprint contest
X	Short game		Offense/Team		Goalkeeper
	Coordination	X	Offense/Series of shots		
	Coordination run		Defense/Individual		**Final part**
	Strengthening		Defense/Small groups	X	Closing game
X	Ball familiarization		Defense/Team		Final sprint
X	Goalkeeper warm-up shooting		Athletics		
			Endurance		

Key:

✖ Cone

🔺 1 Attacking player

🟢 1 Defense player

Ball box

🔴 Medicine ball

Small vaulting box

▬ Foam noodles (foam beams)

Equipment required:
➜ 6-10 cones, one small vaulting box, 6 medicine balls, 1 game of cards, 8 foam noodles (foam beams), 2 ball boxes, each with a sufficient number of handballs

Description:
The objective of this training unit is to improve free play in fast break situations. Following warm-up and a short game, the players play long passes during the ball familiarization phase which will be further developed in the goalkeeper warm-up shooting exercise. This is followed by a series of shots requiring precise passes. Afterwards, the players practice free play in outnumbered, open situations during fast breaks. A closing game with gradually increasing complexity completes this training unit.

The training unit consists of the following key exercises:
- Warm-up/Stretching (individual exercise: 10 minutes/total time: 10 minutes)
- Short game (10/20)
- Ball familiarization (10/30)
- Goalkeeper warm-up shooting (10/40)
- Offense/Series of shots (10/50)
- Offense/Small groups (15/65)
- Offense/Small groups (10/75)
- Closing game (15/90)

Total training time: 90 minutes

No.: 3-1	Warm-up/Stretching	10	10

Course:
- The players make teams of 2, with each team having a ball.
- The players crisscross the gym pairwise while doing different running and passing moves (passing with the throwing hand/non-throwing hand/jump shot passes/wrist passes/passes behind the back).
- After some time, the players gradually increase the distance to each other so that they must play long passes in the end.

Afterwards, the players perform stretching/mobilization exercises together.

No.: 3-2	Short game	10	20

Setting:
- Put medicine balls on the floor in front of each goal line, make two teams.

Course:
- The players initially play team ball in the bottom half of the playing field.
- While doing this, the team in ball possession tries to play five passes in a row, avoiding that the other team wins the ball (A and B).
- The players count the passes loudly.
- If a team manages to play five passes in a row, the players immediately start to run towards the other half of the playing field (C), with the player in ball possession initiating the fast break (D).
- By moving in a well-coordinated manner (E) and passing the ball cleverly (F), the attacking players try to get a player into a good shooting position (G), and to eventually finish the action with a shot at the medicine balls.
- The other team tries to interrupt the fast break (H).

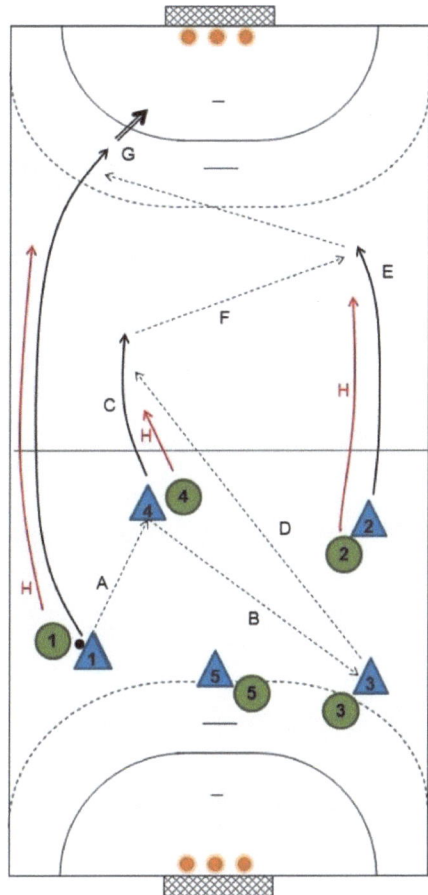

- If the attacking players hit a medicine ball so that it rolls into the goal, they get a point.
- After the shot, the former defending team secures the ball at once and starts to pass it in the upper half of the playing field.
- Which team has scored highest when all of the medicine balls have rolled into the goal or out of the playing field?

⚠ Both teams should quickly adjust and start the subsequent action (fast break/defense) immediately after the fifth pass.

No.: 3-3	Ball familiarization	10	30

Setting:

-   The players make pairs. For each team, position two cones at a large distance to each other (see figure).

Course:

-   ▲2 starts approx. 1 meter in front of his cone and runs in direction of ▲1 (A).

-   ▲1 passes the ball into the running path of ▲2 (B), ▲2 passes back to ▲1.

-   The players play another double pass (C).

-   Afterwards, ▲2 swiftly runs around the cone behind ▲1 (D) and immediately sprints back towards his own cone (E).

-   ▲1 passes the ball into the running path of ▲2 (F).

-   ▲2 dribbles around his own cone at a relaxed pace (G).

-   Afterwards, ▲1 starts the same course, running in direction of ▲2 while playing two double passes. ▲1 runs around the cone behind ▲2, sprints back to his initial position, and receives a long pass from ▲2 into his running path, etc.

-   The other groups do the course in parallel.

-   After five rounds, the players change teammates and repeat the course once more.

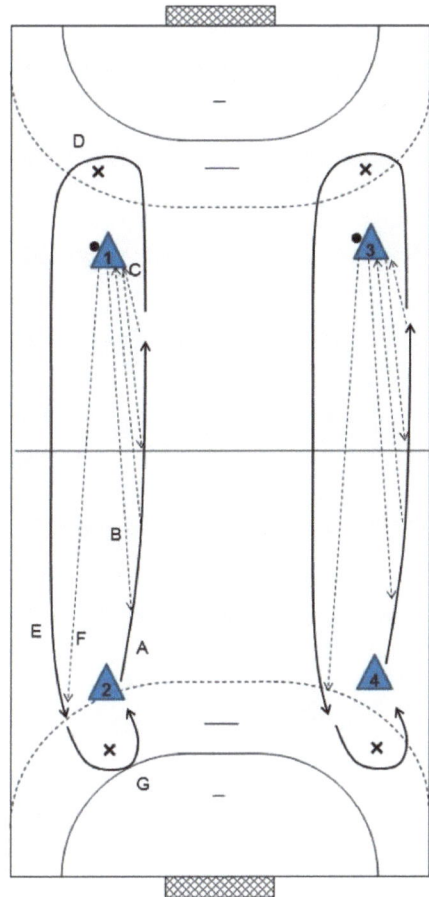

⚠ The players should pass the ball into the running path so that their teammate is able to keep up his speed.

No.: 3-4	Goalkeeper warm-up shooting	10	40

Setting:

- Put medicine balls on the floor in front of the goal line in the bottom half of the playing field and position two ball boxes as shown in the figure.

Course:

- 1 shoots at the left goalpost as instructed (hands, top, bottom) (A); a bit delayed, 2 shoots at the right goalpost (B).

- Afterwards, 3 (to the left) and 4 (to the right) shoot (C and D), etc.

- As soon as the last player has shot from the center (8 in the image), 1 (E) and 2 (F) start to run a fast break.

- The goalkeeper secures one of the balls shot at the goal (G) and initiates the fast break (H). He may choose freely which player will receive the initial pass (1 in the example).

- The other player (2) speeds up while approaching the goal (J),
  and receives a pass into his running path (K).

- 2 shoots and tries to hit a medicine ball so that it rolls into the goal (L).

- The other players (who were not involved in the fast break) each pick up a new ball from the ball boxes and move to the next position on the outer side (M).

- Now the series of shots starts over and over, each time with two players less until all the players have run a fast break.

- Can the players hit all the medicine balls in such a way that they roll into the goal?

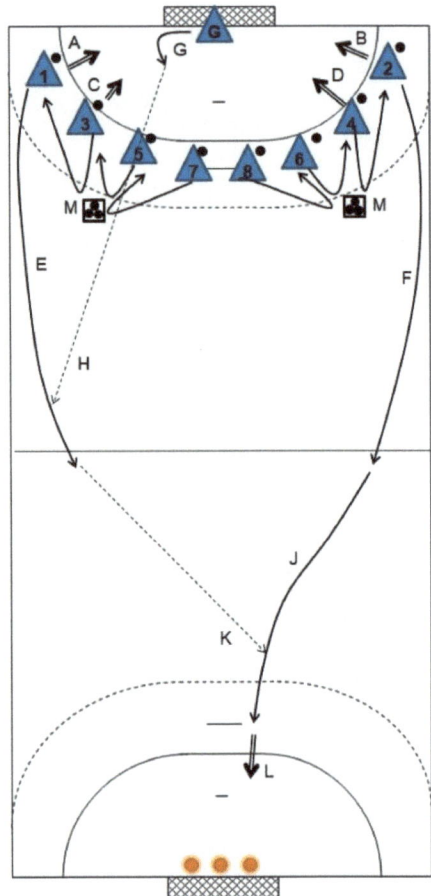

⚠ The goalkeeper should secure a ball immediately after the last shot and initiate the fast break.

No.: 3-5	Offense/Series of shots	10	50

Setting:

- Define the running paths with two cone goals (see figure).

Course:

- **1** passes the ball to the goalkeeper (A), starts a fast break (B), and receives a quick return pass (C) into his running path.

- **1** passes the ball to **2** (D) and runs through the first cone goal.

- **2** passes the ball to **3** (E), at the same time, **1** takes a turn and runs towards the center (F).

- **3** passes the ball into the running path of **1** (G), **1** runs through the second cone goal, and freely shoots at the goal (H).

- Afterwards, **4** starts the next round.

- After his shot, **1** lines up behind **6**; after passing the ball, **3** moves behind **5**; after playing the pass, **2** picks up a new ball and lines up behind **8**.

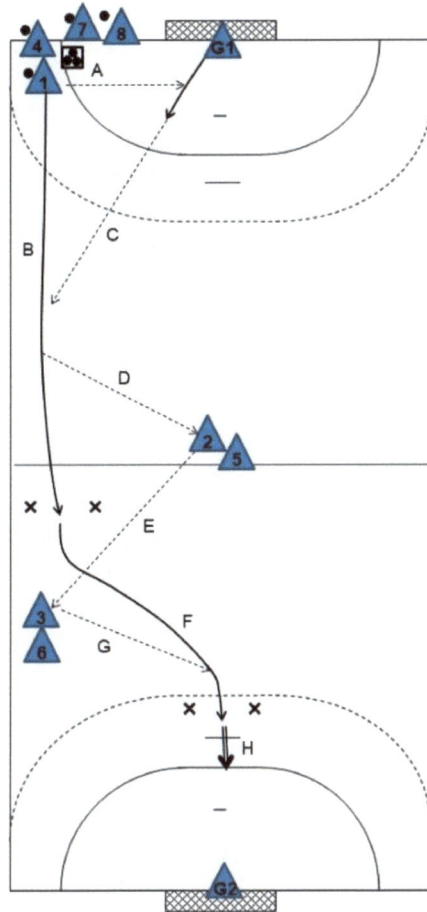

⚠ During the fast break, the players should not slow down when passing and catching the ball; the passes must be played precisely.

⚠ The goalkeepers switch tasks after several rounds.

No.: 3-6	Offense/Small groups	15	65

Setting:
- Position a cone goal on each side next to the goal.
- Put three pairs of foam beams (foam noodles) on the floor next to the 7-meter line and one pair of foam beams on the floor inside the goal (see figure).

Course:
- Three players each (numbers 1-3) stand between two parallel foam beams.
- On command, the players and the goalkeeper start to jump over the left beam and back with their left foot. They shift to the right foot and jump over the right beam and back (A and B), and so on.
- After 5-10 seconds, the coach calls out a number (1, 2, or 3).
- The respective player (1 in the example) immediately starts to run a fast break (C), the goalkeeper picks up one of the balls lying next to the goal (D), and passes the ball to 1 (E).
- 1 shoots at the goal (F).

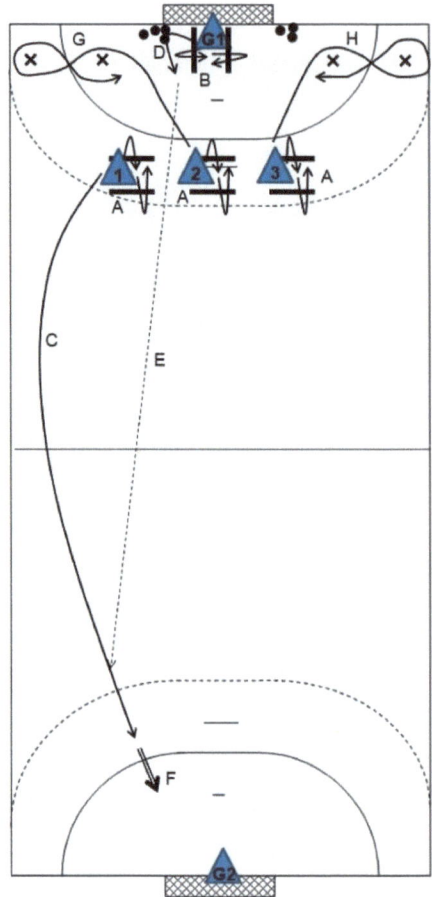

- On the command, the two other players (2 and 3) run to the cone goals on both sides, run around the cones on an "8" path (G and H), and then run through the cone goal again before they also start to run a fast break (J and K).
- The goalkeeper picks up another ball (L) and initiates the fast break (M).
- 1 becomes the defense player after his shot (N).
- 2 and 3 play a 2-on-1 fast break against 1 until one of them has shot at the goal (P and Q).
- Afterwards, three new players start the course over, etc.

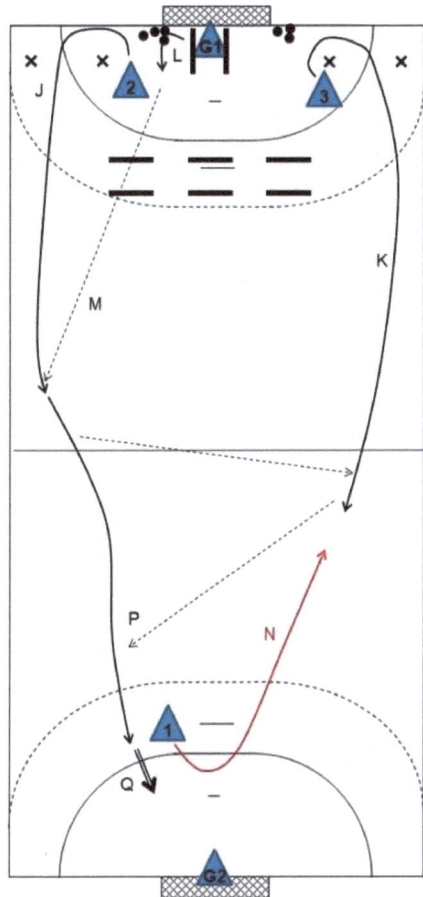

No.: 3-7	Offense/Small groups	10	75

Setting:

- Position a small vaulting box at the center line, divide a game of cards and put both stacks face-down on top of the box.
- Define the starting positions on the other side with two cones (see figure 1).
- Make two teams.

Course:

- One player of each team starts at the small vaulting box, two further players each start at the cones.
- The coach puts a ball on the floor and flips the two upmost cards (A).
- The player with the higher card on the stack (here 1), picks up the ball (B). His team is the attacking team.

⚠️ The other player must not interrupt him.

- 1, 2, and 3 play freely (C, D, and F) against 1, 2, and 3 (E) until one of them has shot at the goal (G).

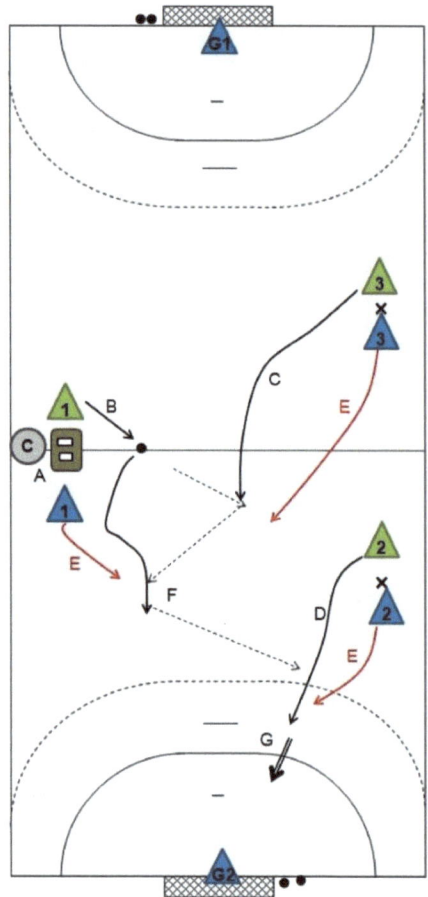

- Immediately after the shot, the players switch tasks, and **1**, **2**, and **3** start to run a fast break towards the other side at once (J in figure 2). The goalkeeper picks up a ball (lying next to the goal) and initiates the fast break (H).
- **1**, **2**, and **3** play freely until one of them has shot at the goal (L and M); **1**, **2**, and **3** try to interrupt the fast break (K).
- Afterwards, new players start the course over.

⚠ In the beginning, the players should quickly recognize which team is the attacking team.

⚠ If the defending players steal the ball, they immediately start a fast break themselves.

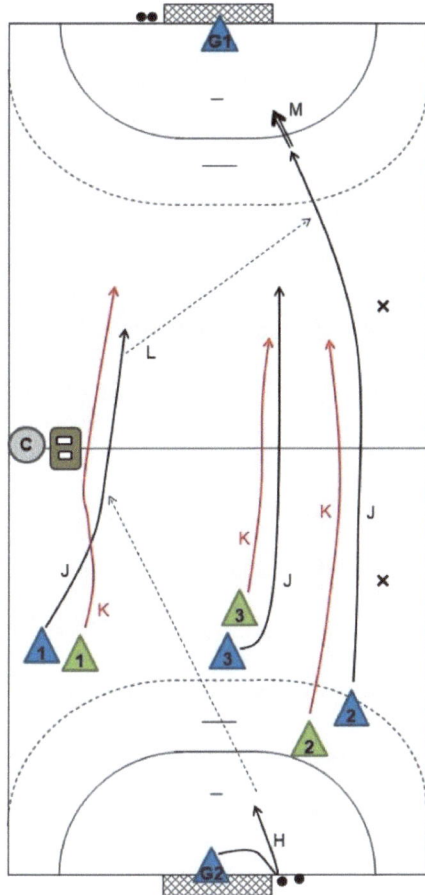

No.: 3-8	Closing game	15	90

Setting:
- Make two teams.

Course:
- 1 starts 1-on-0 with a ball (A) and shoots at any goal without being interrupted (B).
- If 1 misses, another player of the same team may shoot at the other goal.
- If the player scores a goal 1-on-0, another attacking player (C and D) and a defense player (H) enter the game.
- The goalkeeper provides a new ball each time (E and F).
- Now the players play 2-on-1 until another goal is scored (J and K).
- While doing so, the players may substitute (one player leaves the field (G), another one enters the game (C)), but don't have to.

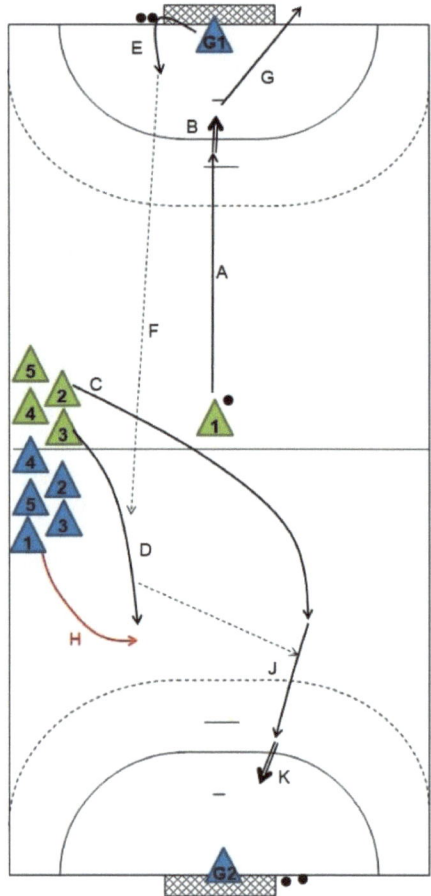

- If a goal is scored 2-on-1, another player per team may enter the game (Q and P); now the players play 3-on-2 (M to S) until the next goal is scored. Further players are added in order to play 4-on-3, 5-on-4, and 5-on-5 in the end.

Overall course:

- One team initially is the attacking team until they have played 5-on-5 (6-on-6 if there are enough players) and scored a goal; afterwards, the players switch tasks and the other team becomes the attacking team. Which team solves the task fastest?
- Players may enter the game only after a goal has been scored (one attacking player, one defense player); otherwise, the number of players remains the same. The players may substitute, however.
- After each attack, the players change the side and approach the other goal.

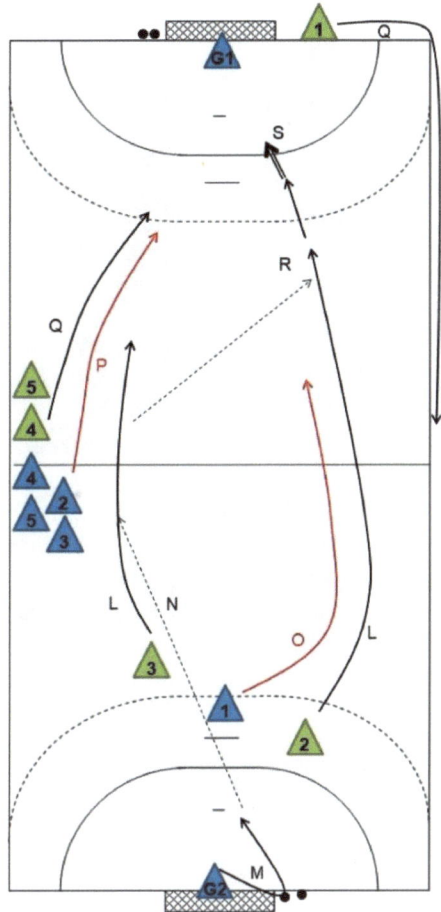

Notes:

_____

_____

_____

_____

_____

_____

No.: 4	Developing a well-structured second wave by implementing long crossing moves and options for further playing		★★★	90
Opening part		**Main part**		
X	Warm-up/Stretching		Offense/Individual		Jumping power
	Running exercise	X	Offense/Small groups		Sprint contest
X	Short game		Offense/Team		Goalkeeper
	Coordination	X	Offense/Series of shots		
	Coordination run		Defense/Individual		**Final part**
	Strengthening		Defense/Small groups	X	Closing game
X	Ball familiarization		Defense/Team		Final sprint
X	Goalkeeper warm-up shooting		Athletics		
			Endurance		

Key:

✖ Cone

△1 Attacking player

●1 Defense player

○ Hoop

▣ Ball box

▢ Small vaulting box

◼ Foam dice

● Medicine ball

Equipment required:
➜ 5 hoops, 12 cones,
1 small vaulting box,
1 foam dice,
2 ball boxes, each with a sufficient number of handballs,
3 medicine balls

Description:

The objective of this training unit is to develop a long crossing during the second wave. Following a warm-up running exercise, a short game, and a ball familiarization exercise, the players initially develop the long crossing during the goalkeeper warm-up shooting phase. In the subsequent series of shots which will be combined with a 1-on-0 fast break, the players practice the long crossing with compensation of the center back player. Defense players and the pivot are added for the two subsequent small group exercises, before the players implement the course 4-on-4 during the closing part of the training unit.

The training unit consists of the following key exercises:
- Warm-up/Stretching (individual exercise: 15 minutes/total time: 15 minutes)
- Short game (10/25)
- Ball familiarization (10/35)
- Goalkeeper warm-up shooting (10/45)
- Offense/Series of shots (10/55)
- Offense/Small groups (15/70)
- Offense/Small groups (10/80)
- Closing game (10/90)

Training unit total time: 90 minutes

No.: 4-1	Warm-up/Stretching	15	15

Setting:

- Put five hoops on the floor of the bottom half of the court, at a short distance to each other. Define the running paths with cones as shown in the figure.

Course 1:

- ▲1 starts dribbling. He should bounce the ball once in each hoop (▲1 runs outside of the line of hoops) (A).
- As soon as he has finished dribbling along the line of hoops, ▲1 speeds up (B) and dribbles around the cones in slalom (C).
- After the last cone, ▲1 sprints around the cone in the center (D) and back to the 6-meter line (E) (70% speed; the players should increase the speed gradually during the further courses, however).
- ▲1 dribbles and sidesteps through the line of cones (F) and touches each cone with the farthermost hand (while taking the ball into the other hand).
- Afterwards, ▲1 lines up again and starts the next round as soon as it is his turn again.
- ▲2 starts as soon as ▲1 has left the line of hoops (A).
- Each player runs (5 to 10) rounds.

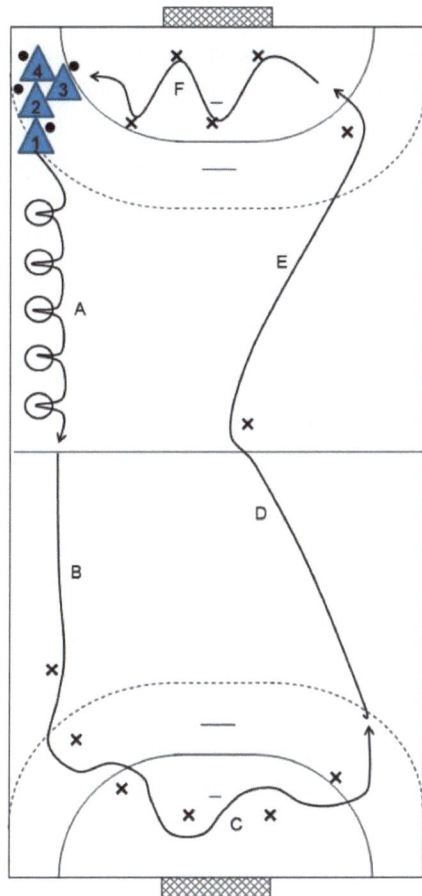

Course 2:

- The initial running path remains the same as in course 1.
- Each player has a second handball.
- The players do the course while dribbling one ball with the hand and the other one with the foot.

- The players do the course while dribbling two handballs at a time. They should bounce one ball into the hoops and the other one with their other hand and as usual (A). In the line of cones (F), the players take up the second ball and touch the cones with it.
- Afterwards, the players perform stretching/mobilization exercises together.

No.: 4-2	Short game	10	25

Setting:
- Make two teams.
- Draw a circle in the center of the court floor or use an already existing circle.
  Put a small vaulting box inside the circle and put a foam dice on top.

Course of action 1:
- One team starts as attacking team. By playing quick passes (A and B), the attacking players try to get into a good shooting position in order to hit the dice on the box (C).
- The other team tries to prevent the attacking team from shooting at the dice; they try to win the ball.
- If they win the ball, the former defending team may try to shoot at the dice on the box themselves.
- The team which hits the dice gets a point.
- Immediately after a team has scored, action 2 starts.

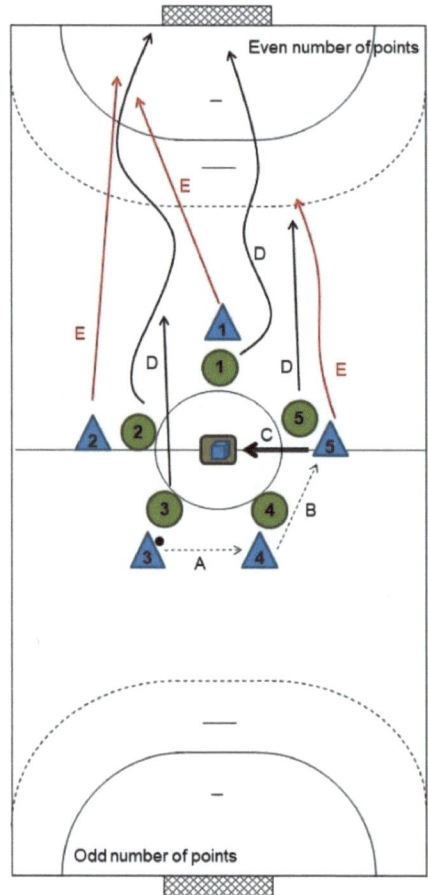

Course of action 2:
- Once the dice has been hit, both teams try to secure the ball (1 succeeds in the figure).
- The number of points on the dice indicates towards which side line the teams play afterwards:
  - If the number of points is odd (1, 3, or 5), the teams play towards the upper side line (as shown in the figure).
  - If the number of points is even (2, 4, or 6), the teams play towards the lower side line.

- The team which won the ball, tries to lay down the ball behind the respective side line as fast as possible (D). If the players succeed, they get a point.
- The other players become the defending team and try to prevent the attacking players from scoring a point (E).

Overall course:
- Count the teams' points scored at the box and at the side line.
- The teams attack and defend alternately in the beginning.
- Which team has scored highest after 20 rounds?

⚠ After the shot at the small box, the players must swiftly secure the ball and start the second action.

No.: 4-3	Ball familiarization	10	35

Setting:

- Position cones as shown in the figure to define the running paths.
- Make two teams.

Course (continuous passing and sprinting):

- ▲1 passes the ball to ▲2 (A), starts to run a fast break (B), and receives a long pass from ▲2 into his running path (C).
- ▲1 dribbles around the backmost cone (D) and plays a double pass with ▲3 while running (E and F).
- During the double pass, ▲4 starts to sprint to the other side (G) and receives a long pass from ▲1 into his running path (H).
- ▲4 plays a diagonal pass to ▲2 (K), who took over the initial position of ▲1 in the meantime (J).
- After playing the pass (H), ▲1 moved to the former position of ▲3 (M), ▲3 moves to the former position of ▲4 (L). ▲4 takes over the former position of ▲2 who will start the next round.
- The second team does the drill in parallel.

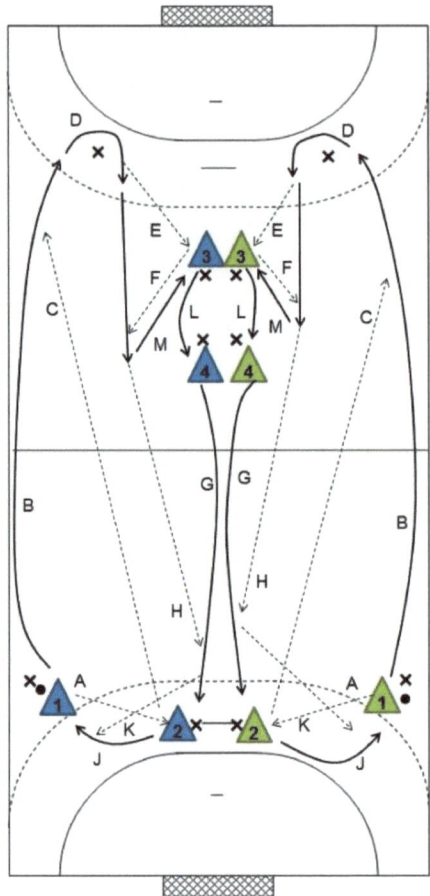

Overall course:

- ▲1 and ▲1 start simultaneously and do the same continuous sprinting and passing exercise (see above).
- The teams repeat the course until each player has run four fast breaks (B).
- Which team has finished the four rounds fastest?

⚠ The players should pass the ball in a precise manner so that they are able to do the drill at high speed. If a ball is lost, the respective player should secure the ball quickly and start the course over at the point where he lost it.

handball-uebungen.de
Trainingseinheiten und Übungen für Ihr Training!

| No.: 4-4 | Goalkeeper warm-up shooting | 10 | 45 |

Setting:
- Put medicine balls on the floor in front of the goal line in the bottom half of the playing field (shooting targets).

Course:
- 1 shoots at the left side of the goal as instructed (hands, top, bottom) (A); 2 shoots at the right side of the goal as instructed, a bit delayed however (B).
- After the shot, both players start to run a fast break (C) (both run past the cones at the outer side).
- G2 passes the ball to 1 at the center line (D).
- 2 speeds up and initiates a long crossing (E). 1 crosses behind 2, receives a pass (F), shoots at the medicine balls, and tries to hit them in such a way that they roll into the goal (G).
- After the shots, 3 and 4 start the same course. However, they should slow down during the fast break so that 1 and 2 have already shot when 3 and 4 start their crossing movements.
- Are the players able to shoot all the medicine balls into the goal until the goalkeeper warm-up shooting is finished?

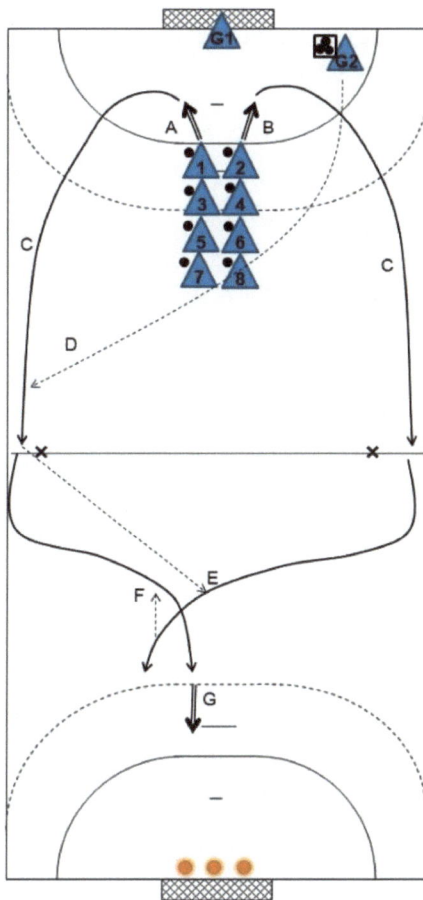

⚠️ The players should speed up considerably during the crossing and find the right timing.

| No.: 4-5 | Offense/Series of shots | 10 | 55 |

Setting:
- Position ball boxes as shown in the figure.

Course:
- 1 passes the ball to G2 (A), starts to run a fast break (B), and receives a long pass from G2 (C) into his running path.
- 1 shoots at the goal (D) and lines up behind 6 with a new ball (figure 2).

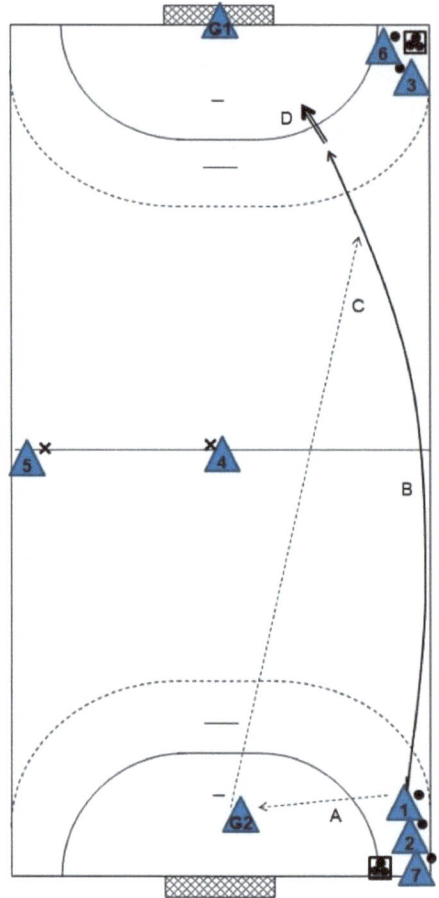

- As soon as 1 has shot, 3 passes the ball to G1 (E), starts to run a fast break (F), and receives a short distance pass from G1 (G).
- 3 passes to 4 (H).
- 5 initiates a long crossing (across the center) (J) and receives a pass into his running path (K).
- 3 speeds up, crosses behind 5 (L), receives a pass into his running path (M), and approaches the goal.
- After playing the pass for the crossing, 4 moves to the position of 5 and approaches the goal in parallel (Q).
- 3 passes the ball into the running path of 4, and 4 shoots at the goal (R).
- Afterwards, 2 starts the next round.
- 4 lines up, 3 takes over the former position of 5, 5 takes over the former position of 4.

⚠️ 5 should initiate a broad crossing movement and vigorously move to the other side (J). 3 should take on the crossing at high speed and approach the goal vigorously.

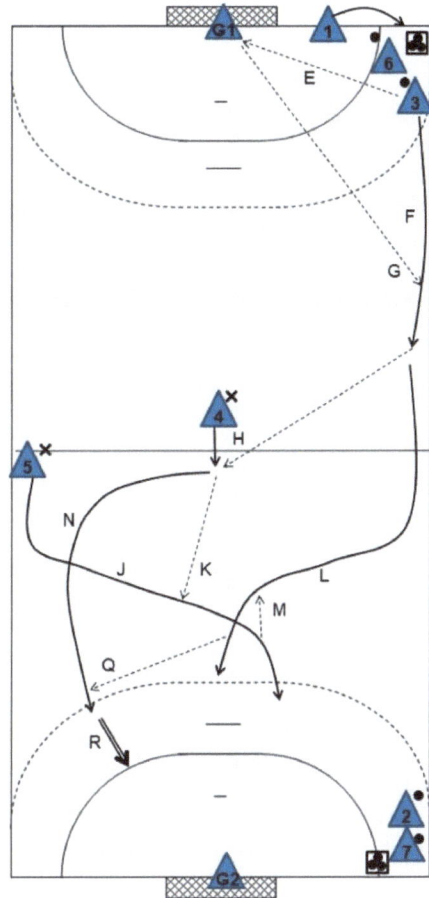

No.: 4-6	Offense/Small groups	15	70

Setting:

- Position ball boxes as shown in the figure.

Course:

- 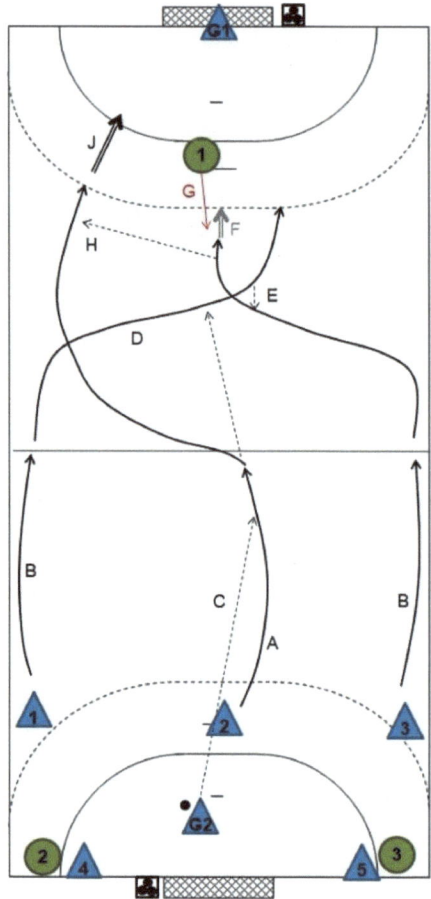 (A), and (B) start to run a fast break (second wave).

- passes the ball to (C).

- initiates a long crossing (across the center) and receives a pass into his running path (D).

- speeds up, crosses behind (E), receives a pass into his running path, and approaches the goal.

- If remains defensive, shoots (F).

- If makes a step forward (G), passes the ball to (H) who moves to the left side and does a parallel piston movement. shoots at the goal (J).

- After the shot, secures the ball (K).

- becomes the new center back player (N) and receives the long pass into his running path (O).

- The two attacking players who did not shoot join the fast break on the left and right side (L and M), the third player becomes the new defense player.

- One player initiates the long crossing and receives a pass from ① into his running path (P).

- ①, ▲1, and ③ play the long crossing 3-on-2 against ② and ③ until one of them has shot at the goal (Q, R, S, and T).

- Afterwards, ②, ③, and ▲4 (as the new teammate) start the course over.

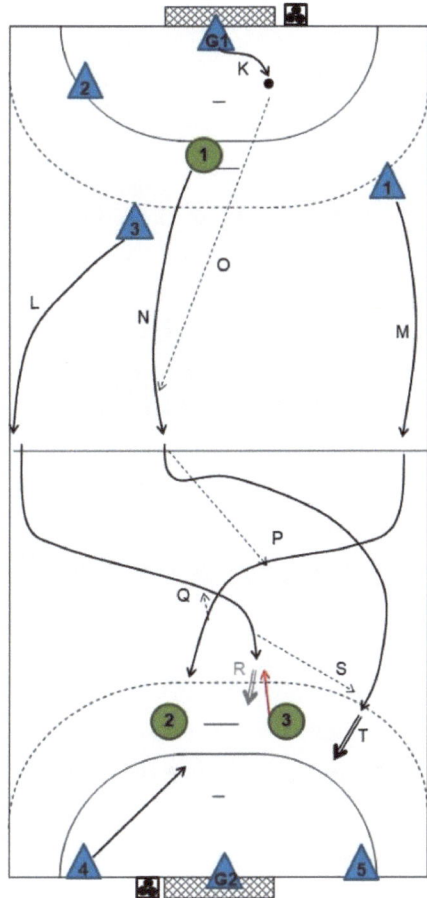

No.: 4-7	Offense/Small groups	10	80

Setting:

- Position ball boxes as shown in the figure.

Course:

- 2, 1, and 3 start to run a fast break (second wave).

- G2 passes the ball to 2 (A).

- One player (here 1) initiates a long crossing (across the center) and receives a pass into his running path (B).

- 3 speeds up, crosses behind 1 (C), receives a pass into his running path, and approaches the goal.

- After the crossing, 1, 2, 3, and the pivot 4 play 4-on-3 in a free game against 1, 2, and 3 until one of them has shot at the goal (D and E).

- Afterwards, G1 immediately secures the ball.

- 4 starts to run a fast break at once and takes over the pivot position on the other half of the playing field again. 1, 2, and 3 become defense players. They should move to the other side immediately.

- 1, 2, and 3 each do three push-ups and then start to run the fast break. G1 passes the ball, and the players repeat the course on the other side.

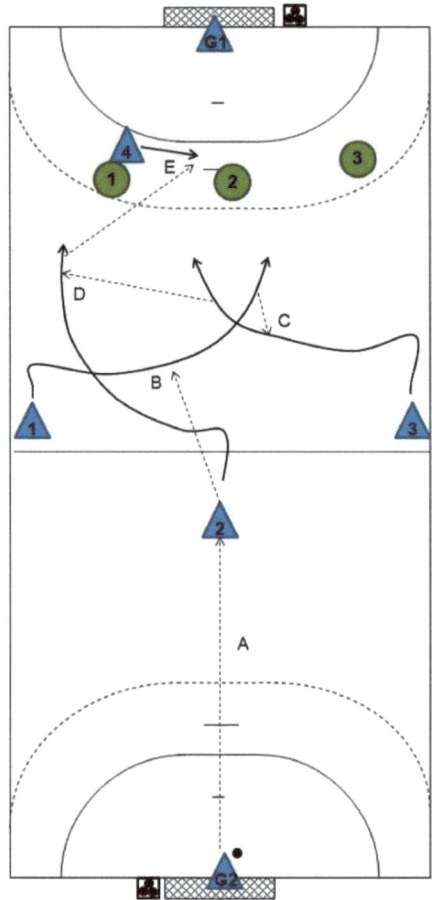

⚠ The players should initiate a broad crossing movement, take on the crossing at top speed, and keep playing freely until one of them has shot at the goal.

⚠ After two rounds, substitute with the remaining players (the shooting player leaves the playing field).

handball-uebungen.de
Trainingseinheiten und Übungen für Ihr Training!

No.: 4-8	Closing game	10	90

Course:

- Two teams play against each other 4-on-4 (5-on-5 or 6-on-6 for more players).
- After each attack (with or without a goal), the defense players start to run a fast break at once.
- The wing players and the pivot run the first wave, the back players start playing the sequence practiced before. The teams keep playing until one of the players has shot at the goal (or lost the ball).
- If a team scores a goal as a direct result of the initial action above, they are allowed a second attack starting from the center line.
- Which team has shot the most goals?

Notes:

_____

_____

_____

_____

_____

_____

_____

_____

_____

_____

_____

_____

_____

No.: 5	Step-by-step development of initial actions after a fast throw-off		★★★	90

Opening part		Main part				
X	Warm-up/Stretching		Offense/Individual			Jumping power
	Running exercise	X	Offense/Small groups			Sprint contest
	Short game	X	Offense/Team			Goalkeeper
	Coordination		Offense/Series of shots			
X	Coordination run		Defense/Individual			**Final part**
	Strengthening		Defense/Small groups	X		Closing game
X	Ball familiarization		Defense/Team			Final sprint
X	Goalkeeper warm-up shooting		Athletics			
			Endurance			

Key:

✖   Cone

▲1   Attacking player

●1   Defense player

▮   Small gym mat

🚧   Hurdle or small vaulting box

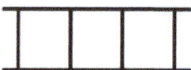

▦   Coordination ladder

Equipment required:
➔ 5 cones, 1 coordination ladder, 2 hurdles (or small vaulting boxes), 1 small gym mat

Description:
The objective of this training unit is to develop a simple initial action after a fast throw-off. Following warm-up and a coordination run exercise, the players practice the basics during the ball familiarization phase and the goalkeeper warm-up shooting. During the three subsequent exercises, the players further develop the running and passing paths and eventually combine them in order to create an initial action. In the closing game, the players implement what they practiced before.

The training unit consists of the following key exercises:
- Warm-up/Stretching (individual exercise: 10 minutes/total time: 10 minutes)
- Coordination run (10/20)
- Ball familiarization (10/30)
- Goalkeeper warm-up shooting (10/40)
- Offense/Small groups (10/50)
- Offense/Team (15/65)
- Offense/Team (15/80)
- Closing game (10/90)

Training unit total time: 90 minutes

No.: 5-1	Warm-up/Stretching	10	10

Course:
- Two players each make a team. Each team has one handball. The teams crisscross the court while easily passing the ball.
- The two players should keep changing the running moves (forward, backward, sidestepping) and the distance to each other.

Extension after a couple of minutes:
- If a team of two has managed to steal another team's ball without losing their own ball, the team that has lost the ball must do five quick jumping jacks, for example. And so on.

The players perform stretching exercises together.

No.: 5-2	Coordination run	10	20

Course 1:

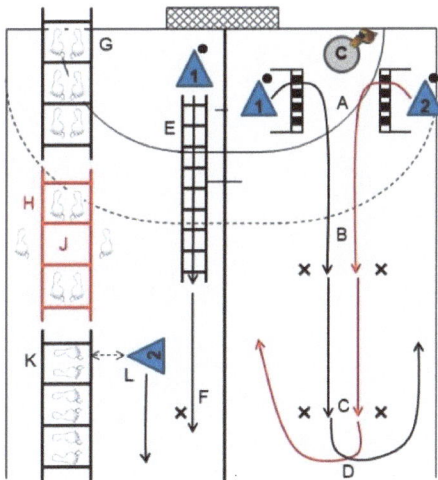

- 1 and 2 stand in front of the hurdle with both feet on the ground and the ball in their hands (face-to-face).
- Once the coach whistles, 1 and 2 start simultaneously, jump over the hurdle (A), and sidestep (facing each other) to the first cone while holding the ball above their head with both hands (B).
- Once they arrive at the cone, both players turn around and sprint forward (dribbling) to the second cone (C). The loser immediately does five quick jumping jacks. Then both players join the line for the next course on the respective other side (D).
- Each player must do three courses on each side.

Afterwards, course 2 begins:

- **1** starts with a ball and runs through the coordination ladder (E); however, he must stick to the following rules:
  - o Run through the coordination ladder as fast as possible, with two footsteps per interspace (left and right) (G), and move the handball around your hips in circles.
- Once **1** arrives at the end of the coordination ladder, he sprints (dribbling) to the cone (F) and then jogs back at slow pace.
- Each player must do two courses.

Further instructions for the next courses:

- Jump through the coordination ladder while doing jumping jacks (H). When your arms meet in the air during the jump movement (J), take the ball in your other hand, etc.
- Sidestep through the coordination ladder with one double-contact per interspace (K) while continuously passing and receiving the ball to/from a teammate (L).

handball-uebungen.de
Trainingseinheiten und Übungen für Ihr Training!

No.: 5-3	Ball familiarization	10	30

Setting:

- The field players line up evenly at the four starting points (at least two players per starting point).

Course:

- ▲1 and ▲3 start the course in parallel. They receive a ball from ▲G1 and ▲G2 into their running paths (A).

- ▲1 and ▲3 should run towards the center line, but keep a slight distance to each other (B) to avoid a crash.

- ▲2 and ▲4 start to run and receive a pass from ▲1 and ▲3 into their running paths towards the goal (C).

- ▲2 and ▲4 pass the ball to ▲G1 and ▲G2 (D). Afterwards, the players repeat the course with passes from the goalkeepers to ▲5 and ▲7; and so on.

- Once they have played the pass, the players should line up at the position to which they passed the ball. ▲2 lines up behind ▲7, ▲4 lines up behind ▲5.

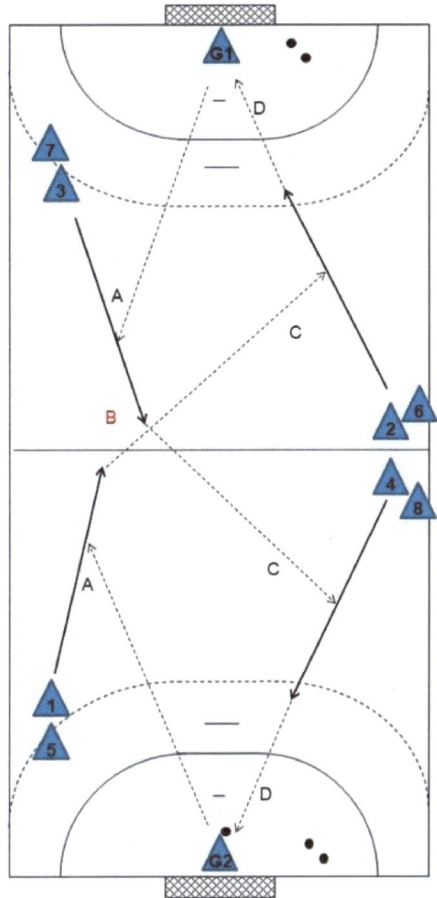

Variants:

- Sprint, catch, pass.
- Jump shot passes only.
- Increase speed.

⚠ Both catch and pass the ball while running, but without dribbling.

⚠ Show "catching hands" to make it easier for the passing player.

⚠ If a ball is lost, the goalkeeper passes a new one immediately.

⚠ Running paths always towards the goal.

| No.: 5-4 | Goalkeeper warm-up shooting | 10 | 40 |

Course:

- 1 approaches the goal with a ball and shoots top left (A).

- 2 approaches the goal a bit delayed and shoots top right (B).

- 3 approaches the goal a bit delayed and shoots bottom left.

- 4 approaches the goal a bit delayed and shoots bottom right.

- After his shot, 4 immediately starts to run to the center line (C).

- G fetches a ball immediately after the last shot (D) and passes it to 4 (E) who waits at the center line in order to catch the ball for the throw-off.

- Afterwards, repeat the course with the next group of four. G should always point at the corner (top left or right) of the first shot:
    - Either: top left – top right – bottom left – bottom right.
    - Or: top right – top left – bottom right – bottom left.

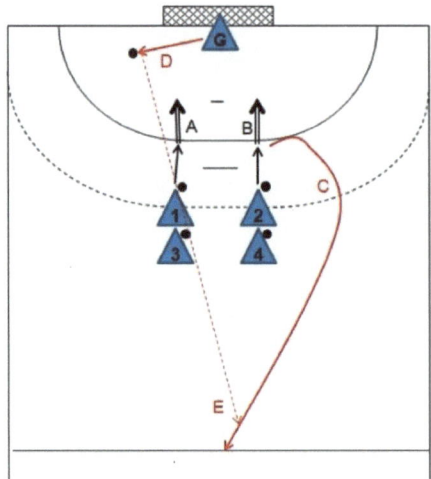

⚠ G should pass the ball to 4 at the center line in such a way that 4 is able to catch it right before the line and step at the defined throw-off point without making more than 1 to 2 steps.

No.: 5-5	Offense/Small groups		10	50

Course:

- G1 starts the course and makes a somersault on the small gym mat (A).

- This is the sign for 1 and 4 to start running (B and C).

- 1 runs to the throw-off point on the center line and, once he has reached the throw-off point, receives a pass from the goalkeeper G1 (D).

- 4 should adjust his speed to stay slightly behind 1 and to keep a certain distance to the center line.

- If 1 stands at the throw-off point correctly according to the rule, the coach whistles (E).

- 4 must now considerably speed up and receives the ball from 1 into his running path (F).

- 4 dribbles around the cone (G), crosses 1 in the center, and passes the ball into the running path of 1 (H).

- 1 shoots at the goal (J).

- Afterwards, 2 and 5 start the same course, etc.

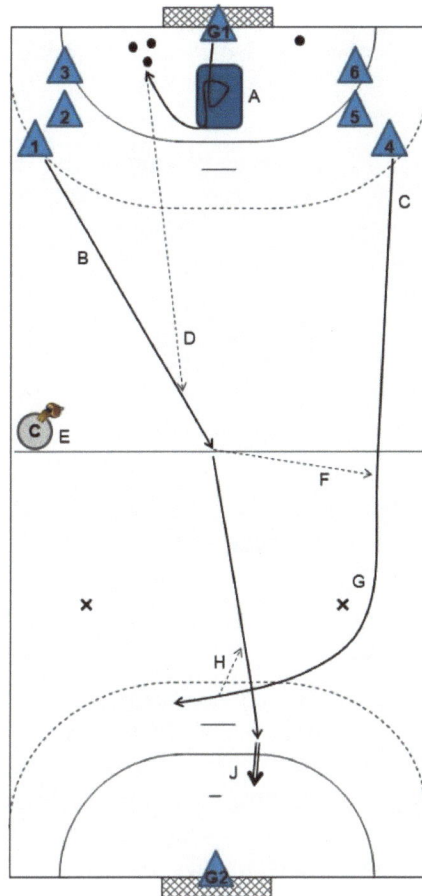

⚠ G1 should pass the ball to the throw-off point (D) in such a way that 1 reaches the throw-off point with one foot after 1 or 2 steps and can then pass the ball immediately after the coach has whistled.

⚠ 4 should coordinate his path towards the center line in such a way that, after the whistle, he can cross the center line at full speed (E) and receive the ball there (F).

No.: 5-6	Offense/Team	15	65

Starting position:

- 1, 2, 3, and 6 stand right behind the 9-meter line, with their faces turned towards the center line.

- 6 serves as feeder/receiver at the center line during the first round.

Course:

- As soon as Ⓒ whistles once, 1, 2, 3, and 6 start to run towards the center line (A). G1 fetches a ball as fast as he can and passes it to 6, in such a way that he can catch it right before the throw-off point and must do no more than one step until he stands on the throw-off point holding the ball according to the rules (C).

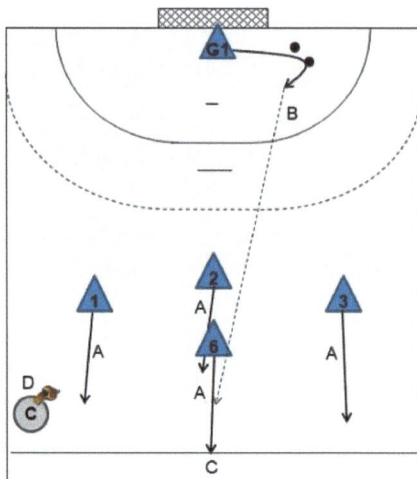

- As soon as 6 stands on the throw-off point properly (C), Ⓒ whistles for the start of play (D).

- 1, 2, and 3 should time their running moves in such a way that they stay behind the center line and are able to cross it at high speed once the coach has whistled (D and E).

- Once the coach has whistled (D), 6 passes the ball into the running path of 1 (F).

- 1 has the ball and dynamically runs through the center and towards 2 while forcing him to move along and towards the left side.

- 3 starts to run a curve (G), takes on the crossing of 1, and receives a pass (H).

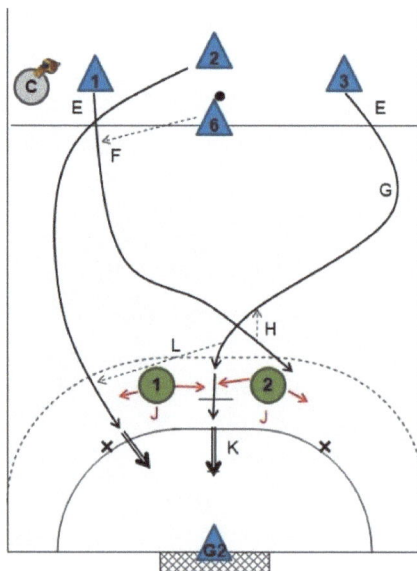

- Depending on the reaction of the defense players 1 and 2 (J), 3 should break through and shoot at the goal (K) or pass the ball to 2 (L), who dynamically runs a long curve and eventually shoots at the goal.
- Afterwards, repeat the course with the next group of four, and so on.
- By playing the pass, 6 decides (F) whether 1 or 3 will initiate the crossing.

⚠ 1, 2, and 3 should always try to break through themselves first. If they don't succeed, they should pass the ball before the defense players interrupt and prevent them from doing so.

⚠ 1, 2, and 3 should do the running moves at high speed following the throw-off.

No.: 5-7	Offense/Team	15	80

Course:

- The initial action, i.e. pass from G1, is the same as in the exercise before (A and B).

- Once C has whistled (C), 6 passes the ball into the running path of either 1 or 3 (D).

- 3 has the ball and dynamically runs through the center (D) and towards 2 while forcing him to move along and towards the wing position.

- 6 keeps on running after the throw-off until he arrives at the 6-meter line (E) and places a screen next to 2, on the inner side (in case of an initial pass to 1, 6 places the screen next to 3).

- 1 starts to run a curve (F), takes on the crossing of 3, and receives a pass (F).

- 1 dynamically approaches the goal with the ball, tries to take advantage of the screening placed by 6, and to break through (G).

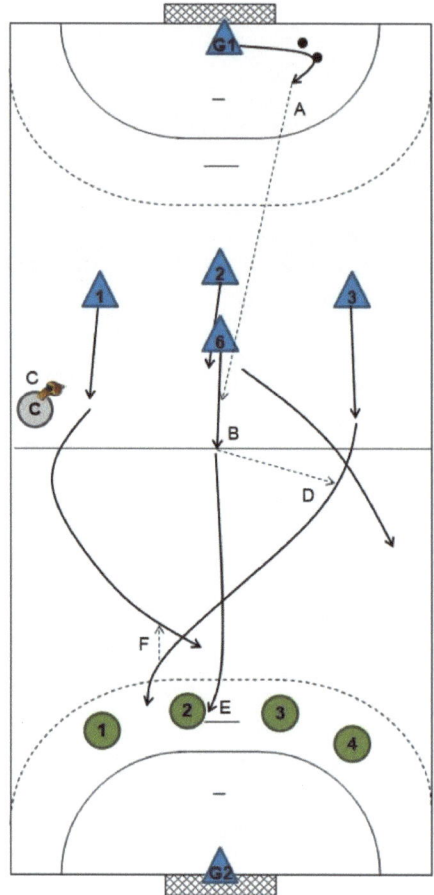

- If ③ obstructs the path for breaking through (G), ▲1 passes the ball to ▲2 (H), who also tries to break through.
- If the attacking players score a goal, the players repeat the course on the other side at once, with ①, ②, ③, and ④ as the new attacking players and a pass from G2 for the throw-off at the center line.
- ▲1, ▲2, ▲3, and ▲4 become the new defense players.
- If the respective attacking players fail to throw at the goal as a result of the fast throw-off, ⓒ whistles anytime during the attack. This is the sign for all the players to switch tasks and to play another fast throw-off.

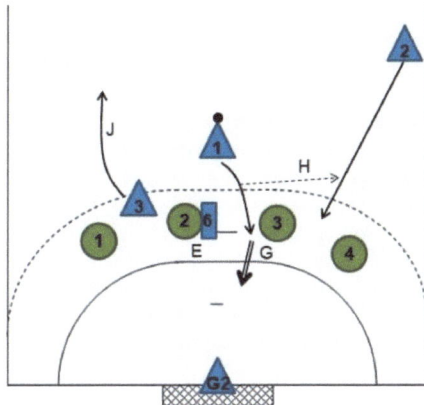

⚠ As soon as they have shot at the goal or as soon as ⓒ has whistled (if the attack lasts too long), the players should start the next attack/defense action at once.

| No.: 5-8 | Closing game | 10 | 90 |

Setting:
- Make two teams. Both teams play 6-on-6 against each other.

Course:
- The players play a fast throw-off after each attack.
- The two wing players should move to their respective positions as fast as they can to be ready for receiving a pass.
- The attacking team may play no more than six passes starting from the center line in order to successfully complete the attack. If they fail to do so, ⓒ whistles and interrupts the attack. The defending team immediately becomes the attacking team playing a fast throw-off, and so on.

The players jog a few minutes and perform stretching exercises together.

5. About the editor

JÖRG MADINGER, born in Heidelberg (Germany) in 1970

July 2014 (further training): 3-day coaching workshop: "Basic components of goalkeeper training", held by the **German Handball Association (Deutscher Handballbund, DHB)**
Lecturers: Michael Neuhaus, Renate Schubert, Marco Stange, Norbert Potthoff, Olaf Gritz, Andreas Thiel, Henning Fritz

May 2014 (further training): 3-day coaching further training during the VELUX EHF Final4, held by the **German Handball Coaching Association (Deutsche Handball Trainer Vereinigung, DHTV)/DHB**
Lecturers: Jochen Beppler (DHB coach), Christian vom Dorff (DHB referee), Mark Dragunski (coach of TuSeM Essen, Germany), Klaus-Dieter Petersen (DHB coach), Manolo Cadenas (coach of the Spanish national team)

May 2013 (further training): 3-day coaching further training during the VELUX EHF Final4, held by the **DHTV/DHB**
Lecturers: Prof. Dr. Carmen Borggrefe (University of Stuttgart, Germany), Klaus-Dieter Petersen (DHB coach), Dr. Georg Froese (sports psychologist), Jochen Beppler (DHB base camp coach), Carsten Alisch (young talents' hockey coach)

Since July 2012: A-License, DHB

Since February 2011: Handball club trainings, coaching (training and competitive areas)

November 2011: Foundation of the Handball Specialist Publishing Company (Handball Fachverlag) (handall-uebungen.de, Handball Practice and Special Handball Practice)

May 2009: Foundation of the handball online platform handball-uebungen.de

2008-2010: Youth coordinator and youth coach, SG Leutershausen (Germany)

Since 2006: B-License

Editor's note
In 1995, a friend convinced me to join him in coaching a handball youth team (male, under 13 years of age).

This was the beginning of my career as a team handball coach. Ever since I enjoyed working as a coach and had high requirements concerning my exercises. Soon, the standard pool of exercises wasn't enough for me anymore and I started to modify and develop drills myself.

Today, I coach a broad range of youth and adult teams with different performance levels and adjust my training units to the individual needs of the teams.

A few years ago, I started selling my exercises and drills online at handball-uebungen.de. Since, in handball training, there is a tendency towards a general athletic training that focuses on coordination work – especially in the training of youth teams –, a large number of my games and exercises can be applied to other sports as well.

Get inspired by the various game concepts, be creative, and rely on your own experiences!

Yours sincerely,
Jörg Madinger

6. Further reference books published by DV Concept

From warm-up to handball team play – 75 exercises for every handball training unit

By making your training units more diverse, you can increase the players' motivation, since you consistently offer new approaches to improve and refine familiar movement sequences. In this book, you will find inspiring exercises you can apply during each phase of your everyday team handball training – from warm-up and goalkeeper warm-up shooting to the common contents of the main phase and the closing games. Each exercise is illustrated and described in an easy, comprehensible manner. Specific notes give you tips on what you need to be aware of.

This book deals with the following key subjects:

Warm-up:
- Basic warm-up
- Short warm-up games
- Sprint contests
- Coordination
- Ball familiarization
- Goalkeeper warm-up shooting

Basic exercises, basic play, and target play:
- Offense/series of shots
- General offense
- Fast throw-off
- 1st and 2nd wave
- Defensive action
- Closing games
- Endurance

At the end of this book, you will find an entire methodological training unit. The objective of this training unit is to improve shooting and quick decision-making under pressure.

Minihandball training and handball training for young kids (5 training units)

Minihandball training and handball training for kids is different from handball training for older players and considerably different from handball training for competitive players. During their first contact with "handball", kids should be familiarized with the ball in a playful way. They should be taught that being active, doing sports, playing together, and even playing against each other is fun.

This book contains a short introduction to handball for kids and young children and its special characteristics as well as example exercises which help to make your training units interesting and more diverse.

Following this, there are five complete training units of different difficulty levels that focus on the basic handball techniques (dribbling, passing, catching, shooting, and defending in a game with opponents). The kids are playfully introduced to the subsequent handball-specific basics. At the same time, particular attention is payed to general physical experience and the development of coordination skills.

The exercises are illustrated and described in an easy, comprehensible manner. They can be immediately integrated in every training unit. By using the given training variants, you can easily adjust the difficulty level of the training units to the respective target group. The variants should also encourage you to modify and further develop the exercises to make each training unit a new and more diverse experience for the children.

Passing and catching while moving – 60 exercises for each handball training unit
Passing and catching are two basic handball techniques which must be trained and improved continuously. These 60 practical exercises offer you various options to train passing and catching in a challenging and diverse manner. The exercises particularly focus on improving passing and catching skills even during highly dynamic movements. The drills therefore combine new running paths and movements similar to real game situations.

The exercises are illustrated and described in an easy, comprehensible manner. They can be immediately integrated in every training unit. Various difficulty and complexity levels allow for adjustment of the passing and catching drills to each age group.

Effective goalkeeper warm-up shooting – 60 exercises for every handball unit
Goalkeeper warm-up shooting is essential for almost every training unit. These 60 warm-up shooting exercises provide you with a variety of ideas to make the warm-up shooting challenging and diverse, both for the goalkeepers and the field players. The exercises particularly focus on improving the players' dynamics even during the warm-up shooting.

The exercises are illustrated and described in an easy, comprehensible manner. They can be immediately integrated in every training unit. Whether you combine the exercises with additional coordination drills or use them as an introduction to the main part – various difficulty levels allow for adjustment of the warm-up shooting to each training unit and age group.

Competitive games for your everyday handball training – 60 exercises for each age-group

Handball needs quick and correct decisions in each game situation. This can be trained playfully and diversely through handball-specific games. These 60 exercises are divided into seven categories and train the playing skills.

The book deals with the following subjects:
- Team ball variants
- Team play with different targets
- Tag games
- Sprint and relay race games
- Ball throwing and transportation games
- Games from other types of sports
- Complex closing game variants

The exercises are illustrated and described in an easy, comprehensible manner. They can be immediately integrated in every training unit. Various difficulty levels, additional notes, and possible variations allow for adjustment to each age group.

Paperback from the Handball Practice series (Handball Praxis) (five training units each)

Handball Practice 9 – Basic offense training for players aged 9 to 12 years

Handball Practice 11 - Extensive and diverse athletics training

Handball Practice 14 - Interaction of back position players with the pivot – Shifting, Screening, and Using the Russian Screen

Special Handball Practice 1 - Step-by-step training of a 3-2-1 defense system

Special Handball Practice 2 - Step-by-step training of successful offense strategies against the 6-0 defense system

For further reference and e-books visit us at:

www.handball-uebungen.de

www.ingramcontent.com/pod-product-compliance
Lightning Source LLC
Chambersburg PA
CBHW042129080426
42735CB00001B/16